contents

CULTURE SMART!

BELARUS

Anne Coombes

·K·U·P·E·R·A·R·D·

First published in Great Britain 2008
by Kuperard, an imprint of Bravo Ltd
59 Hutton Grove, London N12 8DS
Tel: +44 (0) 20 8446 2440 Fax: +44 (0) 20 8446 2441
www.culturesmartguides.com
Inquiries: sales@kuperard.co.uk

Culture Smart! is a registered trademark of Bravo Ltd

Distributed in the United States and Canada
by Random House Distribution Services
1745 Broadway, New York, NY 10019
Tel: +1 (212) 572-2844 Fax: +1 (212) 572-4961
Inquiries: csorders@randomhouse.com

Series Editor Geoffrey Chesler
Design Bobby Birchall

ISBN 978 1 85733 472 2

British Library Cataloguing in Publication Data
A CIP catalogue entry for this book is available from the
British Library

Printed in Malaysia

Cover image: Castle in Mir. © *Sleepinsun/Dreamstime.com*
Images on pages 29 (top), 51, 52, 53, 66, 94, 98, 101, 103, and 105 by courtesy of the author.
Images on pages 13, 29 (bottom), 43, 88, 96, 122 (bottom), 130, 141, and 143 © Hanna
Zelenko; 21 © Monk; 37 © 32X; 87 © Andrey Bondar; 104 Szeder László;
119 © diasUndKompott; 122 (top) © Giancarlo Rosso; 123 © Ihar; 127 © Redline;
137 © Torarne; 140 © Alex Zelenko; and 164 © Viktar Palsciuk.

About the Author

ANNE COOMBES edits the English-language editions of Belarusian state publications such as the *Minsk Times*, *Belexport Magazine*, and the *Foreign Economic Review*. She also works as a copy editor for the International Finance Corporation and the United Nations Development Programme in Belarus (IFC is part of the World Bank) in addition to editing the English pages of the *Where Minsk* city guide. She spent three years in Minsk, where her husband was posted as a diplomat, and now lives in the USA, working as a copywriter and travel journalist.

**The Culture Smart! series is continuing to expand.
For further information and latest titles visit
www.culturesmartguides.com**

The publishers would like to thank **CultureSmart!**Consulting for its help in researching and developing the concept for this series.

CultureSmart!Consulting creates tailor-made seminars and consultancy programs to meet a wide range of corporate, public-sector, and individual needs. Whether delivering courses on multicultural team building in the USA, preparing Chinese engineers for a posting in Europe, training call-center staff in India, or raising the awareness of police forces to the needs of diverse ethnic communities, it provides essential, practical, and powerful skills worldwide to an increasingly international workforce.

For details, visit www.culturesmartconsulting.com

CultureSmart!Consulting and **CultureSmart!** guides have both contributed to and featured regularly in the weekly travel program "Fast Track" on BBC World TV.

contents

Map of Belarus

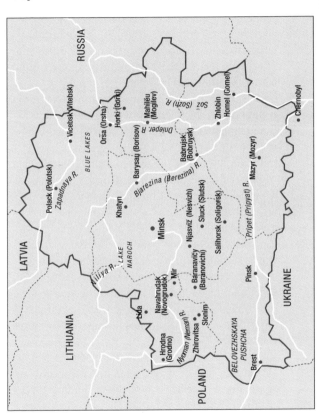

introduction

Belarus has been much in the news in recent
years. Its president is widely derided as Europe's
"last dictator" and many think of it as a rather
backward, insignificant country on the outer edge
of our Western world. A stroll through the capital,
Minsk, is often said to be like stepping fifty years
back in time. It's not hard to imagine Soviet tanks
rolling down the main avenue. It is more than just
the architecture that harks back to this bygone
age, though: try navigating the official
bureaucracy, or getting waited on in a shop!

Belarus may have been long under the Russian
thumb—and many of the older generation still
feel strong ties to their "Soviet Fatherland"—but
it is far from being a carbon copy of its neighbor.
Centuries of "outside" rule have bred a form of
stoicism that, among older people, borders on
fatalism. Nevertheless, the Belarusians have their
own quiet pride in their land and the young are
passionately patriotic, wanting to carve out an
identity separate from Russia. Many traditions are
shared with the Russians, but most Minskers
would laugh at any comparison to Muscovites,
whom they largely regard as materialistic and
aggressive. While Moscow's culture and power are
admired and respected, they are well aware that
their Russian cousins consider them provincial.

Belarus occupies a key geographical position
on the strategic crossroads from East to West,
between Moscow and Warsaw, Vilnius and Kiev.
For centuries, armies have trudged across its

plains, wreaking destruction. Now, it likes to think of itself as the ideal trade route—which it might be, were it not for the arcane customs procedures at the border.

Belarus's leadership has hitherto thrown in its lot with Russia; for almost a decade, they have been planning a Union State. However, the relationship has soured in the last couple of years, particularly since Gazprom began charging higher prices for its gas and oil. The president is now making overtures to the EU as never before, and the EU continues to urge him to respect human rights and introduce real democracy. A quick Internet search turns up stories of journalists and political figures who mysteriously disappear, of opposition party members imprisoned on apparently trivial charges, and a hair-raising catalog of alleged human rights abuses.

Regardless of their views on its leadership, few visitors leave Belarus without falling in love with it a little. Their conservative social views may leave something to be desired, but the people are disarmingly friendly, and you can't help admiring their resilience, bravery, and resourcefulness. Come what may—Second World War devastation, Stalin's purges, or the cruel post-*perestroika* years—they gird their loins and hang in there. In addition, they are spontaneous, thoughtful toward others, and love a good party. They work their way into your heart.

Pryvita ne! Welcome to Belarus!

Key Facts

Official Name	Republic of Belarus (*Respublika Byelarus'*)	
Capital City	Minsk (population 1.8 million)	
Major Cities	Gomel, Grodno, Mogilev, Brest, and Vitebsk	
Area	80,155 sq. miles (207,600 sq. km)	A little smaller than Great Britain
Borders	Latvia, Lithuania, Poland, Russia, and Ukraine	
Climate	Moderately continental, between maritime and continental.	Over the last decades winters have become warmer.
Currency	Belarusian ruble (BRb)	Exchange rate US $1 = 2,135 BRb; GB £1 = 4,229 BRb (May 2008)
Population	9,689,700 in 2007 (state statistics)	47 people per sq. km, with 72 % in urban areas
Ethnic Distribution	Belarusian 81.2%, Russian 11.4%, Polish 3.9 percent, Ukrainian 2.4 %, other 1.1% (1999 census)	
Language	Belarusian and Russian are the official national languages.	
Religion	Mainly Eastern Orthodox Christian (80 percent)	Other religions: Roman Catholic, Protestant, Jewish, and Muslim

Government	President is Head of State. The National Assembly consists of the Council of the Republic (64 seats; 56 elected by regional councils and 8 appointed by the president) and the Chamber of Representatives (110 seats, elected by universal adult suffrage).	There are 6 oblasts (administrative provinces) – Brest, Gomel, Grodno, Minsk, Mogilev, and Vitebsk, and one municipality—the capital of Minsk.
Media	State-run media dominates. Treatment of independent media has brought criticism from the EU and various media watchdogs.	Local TV channels broadcast mainly in Russian; the picture is often of poor quality due to shared aerials. International satellite is available in the top hotels.
Electricity	220 volts, 50 Hz	Standard two-prong plug (adapters needed)
Video/TV	PAL/SECAM system	NTSC TV does not work in Belarus.
Radiation	Levels in affected areas are monitored. An exclusion zone is in operation.	The rest of the country is considered "safe" by the authorities.
Telephone	The international dialing code is +375. The code for Minsk is 17.	To dial out of Belarus, dial 8 (for outside the city) then 10, followed by the country code.
Internet Domain	.by	
Time Zone	GMT + 2 hours	In summer, clocks go forward one hour.

chapter one

LAND & PEOPLE

GEOGRAPHICAL SNAPSHOT

Belarus is a landlocked country in Eastern Europe, bordering Latvia, Lithuania, Poland, Russia, and Ukraine. It likes to boast that it is at the center of Europe, ideally positioned as a transit corridor for East–West trade. In some ways, this is true. Russia has been piping gas to Europe through Belarus for some time now. However, this arrangement is currently under some strain as Russia seeks to phase out the subsidies it has traditionally granted Belarus, in favor of charging more realistic prices for its products. Belarus can ill afford to pay market prices for its fuel and has used its power to interrupt the transit of supplies as a bargaining chip.

If you drive across Belarus, you'll see that it's quite flat, with many forests, lakes and swamps. Around 27 percent of the land is farmed. The major expressways are kept in fair condition, but, as you might expect, the less used rural thoroughfares are quite potholed. Winters are generally cold and snowy; 14°F is usual (–10°C) but temperatures can dip to –22°F (–30°C) on occasion. Spring and fall are rainy and cool, at 50–60°F (10–15°C), while summer is humid, with temperatures easily hitting 70°F (21°C), with occasional spurts up to 90°F (32°C).

Chernobyl

Reactor Number 4 at the Chernobyl nuclear power plant in northern Ukraine exploded on April 26, 1986. The measure of radiation released by the explosion was more than a hundred times that experienced by Hiroshima and Nagasaki, and Belarus lay directly in the path of danger, with winds blowing the fallout straight over the border. The south and southeast of the country remain particularly affected by radiation, having received around 70 percent of the total fallout. Infant mortality in affected areas is 20 percent above the national average, and two-thirds of all infant deaths are attributable to abnormal fetal development.

Initially, local people were kept largely in the dark over what had happened, and several days passed before evacuation began from the affected areas; most believed they would be returning. Of course, all the possessions they left behind were contaminated, so could never be recovered.

Limited information was shared on the consequences to health. Naturally, many felt that they had been misled by the authorities.

The longer-term social and psychological effects have been significant. Incidences of depression and alcohol dependence in affected areas have risen, exacerbated by a lack of employment opportunities and a sense of fatalism. Many women from the region have long been scared of having children, fearing abnormalities, and those who move away usually try to keep their former home secret, anxious that men won't marry them. The Belarusian government is now implementing a revival plan to set up factories and provide modern housing, schools, and hospital facilities in the affected areas, addressing a desperate need. Gradually, hope is returning.

More than 80 percent of human radioactive contamination is thought to be caused by eating contaminated food, rather than exposure to the environment. Concern remains over the health of children (occurrence of thyroid cancer is particularly high), but experts are divided on long-term consequences for the population. 1.3 million reside in the Gomel and Mogilev regions, the most contaminated, with respectively 64 percent and 30 percent of their total areas affected, according to state statistics. A fifth of all farming land has been affected, and agriculture is still forbidden in parts of the south.

In the exclusion zone, the wilderness has returned, with wolves and other wildlife roaming free. According to state figures, a total area of around 60,000 square miles (around 155,000 sq. km) is still contaminated, and will remain so for most of the next century. More than 770 square miles (more than 2,000 sq. km) of forest are affected, so eating berries or mushrooms from them is ill-advised. As radionuclides slowly penetrate the soil they filter down into the water table and poison rivers and lakes—the water supply for thousands of people. Domestically produced food available in cities is regularly checked for radiation by the authorities and is generally declared to be at "reasonable" levels.

Agencies such as the United Nations Development Programme in Belarus have been working to improve the quality of life of those living in affected areas, from supporting ventures and training schemes that will enhance job opportunities for local people to showing them which foods are most likely to be contaminated and how to use radiation detecting equipment. In addition, a vast number of international charity groups (many based in Italy, Ireland, and the UK) have been working to improve the lives of young people in these regions. Some children travel abroad on recuperative trips. Hands-on help and financial funding have also been given to improve housing, health, and education facilities in affected settlements. The Belarusian government has been keen to accept support in alleviating the consequences of the Chernobyl catastrophe.

Population Decline

The country has a population of around ten million, having steadily declined between 1993 and 2001 at around 50,000 annually. This was largely due to deaths exceeding births, in addition to the emigration of young Belarusians. The

government is now actively promoting family life— advocating that it is every young woman's duty to have at least three children (2005 UNESCO figures showed that the average was 1.2 births per woman). Various child benefits are being offered to encourage this trend.

In the late 1990s, almost two-thirds of pregnancies ended in abortion, while a significant number of babies were abandoned to orphanages. Teenagers' lack of sex education and access to contraceptives is partly to blame but many of these unwanted pregnancies happened to families who felt they simply could not cope with another child to look after, bearing in mind that most live in very small apartments and have limited incomes. Women living in Chernobyl-affected areas also feared for the health of their unborn children. The president has warned that low birth rates are a potential threat to sustainable economic development. On a positive note, state figures show that the birthrate rose by 6.5 percent in 2006 and abortions fell to around one in three pregnancies. In 2007, the birthrate rose by a further 7.3 percent and mortality rates fell by 4 percent, resulting in a population fall of 3 percent.

The 2006 Independence Day parade included all those who had recently wed, resplendent in their beautiful wedding outfits. The campaign to promote marriage and family life was evident in 2006, proclaimed "The Year of the Mother," and continued in 2007 with "The Year of the Child," and in 2008 with "The Year of Health." As mortality levels begin to stabilize and birthrates rise, for the first time in a decade, it seems that positive population growth is within reach.

Young people in rural areas are increasingly heading for cities in search of opportunities: 73.4 percent of the population now live in urban surroundings. Around 30 percent of villagers are over sixty years of age. Additionally, women of childbearing age (15–49) made up just 21.5 percent of rural residents in 2005. The government is countering this by allocating significant funding to the development of agriculture and industry in rural areas, to promote employment and living standards.

A BRIEF HISTORY

Belarusians have only recently begun to think of themselves and function as an independent nation. Historically, they were passed from one neighbor to another—marched over, annexed, and dominated. This legacy helps to explain their characteristic traits of stoicism and acceptance.

Belarusian roots go back to the Slavic migrations into Eastern Europe between the sixth and eighth centuries, into territories already settled by Baltic tribes. They are mostly descended from East Slavic tribes—the Dregovichs, Krivichs, and Radimichs—some of whom mixed with the local Balts. The Slavs were pagan, agrarian people who traded in agricultural produce, game, furs, honey, beeswax, and amber. During the ninth and tenth centuries, the Varangians, Viking invaders, established trading posts along the waterways linking Scandinavia to the Byzantine Empire, crossing the lakes and rivers of modern-day Belarus. This became a lucrative trade route and gradually the Varangians assumed sovereignty over the East Slavic tribes. In time they assimilated into the majority Slavic population.

The Principality of Polotsk

The first East Slavic state, Kievan Rus, emerged in the tenth century—a loose network of principalities along the trade routes from the Baltic to the Black Sea. Its major centers were Novgorod (in Russia), Polotsk (in northern Belarus), and Kiev (in Ukraine). Polotsk, on the Dvina River, was the dominant power on Belarusian territory, often asserting its independence within the grouping. It was also the first city in Belarus to embrace Christianity—in 992—via the Greek Orthodox Church, under the Metropolitan of Kiev. Nevertheless, pagan rituals and beliefs continued to flourish for many centuries.

Litva—The Grand Duchy of Lithuania

After the destruction of Kievan Rus by the Tatars in 1240, the principality of Polatsk was subsumed into the Grand Duchy of Lithuania, thus helping to shape Lithuania's political, religious, and cultural life. The Belarusian language, which had begun to form in the first half of the thirteenth century, became the official language of the Grand Duchy, a situation that lasted from the mid-fourteenth to the late-seventeenth century, when it was replaced by Polish.

In order to protect Lithuania from the depredations of the Teutonic Knights, whose ostensible mission was the conversion of the pagan peoples of Eastern Europe, in 1385 the Grand Duchy joined Poland in a dynastic union, thereby creating the largest country in Europe. The pagan Grand Duke Jogaila was baptized into the Catholic Church in order to marry Jadwiga, the heir to the Polish throne, and Roman Catholicism became the state religion.

In 1410, at the great Battle of Grünwald, the united armies of Poland and Lithuania decisively defeated the Teutonic Knights, and a period of prosperity followed. Royal charters confirmed the equality of Catholic and Orthodox feudal lords. The Lithuanian and Belarusian nobility, however, started converting to Catholicism and adopting Polish culture, and the Orthodox Belarusian peasantry came to be ruled by a class that shared neither their language nor their religion. The

native, self-governing Orthodox Church came
under pressure from the Polish authorities to
unite with Rome. Moscow began to assert itself as
the defender of Orthodoxy throughout Eastern
Europe, particularly after the fall of
Constantinople to the Turks in 1453.

The Polish–Lithuanian Commonwealth

In 1569, by the Union of Lublin, the Grand Duchy
of Lithuania and the Kingdom of Poland formed
a federal state with a single Sejm
(parliament)—the Polish–Lithuanian
Commonwealth. This covered modern-
day Poland, Lithuania, Belarus, Latvia,
large parts of Ukraine and Estonia, and
some parts of western Russia. Polish
culture and language permeated
Belarus, and Polish or Polonized nobles
ruled the land. With the dying out of the
Jagiellonian dynasty, the Polish monarchy became
elective; central government grew weak, and the
power of the nobility increased, leading to
infighting and political instability.

Political conflict was fueled by religion. In the
sixteenth century the Protestant Reformation
introduced Lutheranism and Calvinism to
Belarus. The Counter-Reformation spearheaded
by the Jesuits brought fanatical persecution of all
non-Catholics. In 1596 the Uniate Church was
formed to reconcile the Orthodox and fend off
Moscow. This was a union of the native Orthodox
Church with the Catholic Church, by which the

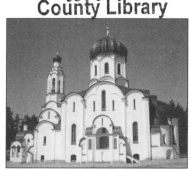

Orthodox broke their links with the Patriarch of Constantinople and acknowledged the supremacy of the Pope, accepting certain articles of Catholic doctrine in return for retaining their traditional rites and a measure of autonomy. In the event, many of the Orthodox faithful rejected this compromise and the native Orthodox Church continued to exist alongside the Uniate Church.

The Polish–Lithuanian state's ferocious oppression of the native Orthodox Church gave Moscow the opening it needed to further its imperial ambitions. From 1648 to 1654 there was a peasant uprising against Polish landowners, and many Belarusians fled to Ukraine to join the Russian-backed Cossack rebellion.

From 1654 to 1667, Russia invaded and occupied a large portion of Belarus, creating a demographic and economic crisis. Cities were destroyed and about half the population was killed, including 80 percent of the urban population. The Great Northern War of 1700–21, a struggle between Russia and Sweden for control of the Baltic, in which Poland–Lithuania was allied with Russia, was a further disaster for

Belarus. Political anarchy and religious divisions within the country gave its powerful neighbors the opportunity they wanted.

Imperial Russia

In 1772, 1793, and 1795 the enfeebled Polish–Lithuanian state was partitioned by Russia, Prussia, and Austria, after which the whole of Belarus was incorporated into the Russian Empire. Minsk was designated the regional capital.

In 1794, the Belarusian-born nobleman Tadeusz Kosciuszko (who had trained in France and was a hero of the American Revolutionary War) led an uprising against the Russian occupation, which was soon suppressed. A monument stands to him in Lafayette Square, opposite the White House in Washington.

Napoleon's Grande Armée crossed the border of the Russian Empire in 1812. He was defeated and forced to retreat with terrible losses. A significant rearguard battle took place at the Berezina River in Belarus as the French army attempted to cross its bridges; the remains of French soldiers are still being unearthed today and given a Christian burial.

Apart from the destruction he wreaked, Napoleon's legacy was the dissemination of democratic ideas allied to nationalism. In 1830–31 a national-liberation uprising to restore Poland–Lithuania within the 1772 boundaries broke out. It failed to gain the support of the peasants in the countryside, however, and was decisively crushed. The political and economic power of the Polish-Catholic establishment was broken and the legal status of the Duchy of Lithuania was annulled. Few educated Belarusians now held positions of influence, while the Belarusian masses were generally regarded as provincial peasants.

Russification, Resistance, and the Emergence of a Modern Identity

As part of the crackdown, the Tsarist regime inaugurated an intensive program of de-Polonization and Russification. National cultures, including Belarusian, were repressed, those who had converted to Roman Catholicism were pressed to reconvert to Orthodoxy, and native Orthodox believers were forced to accept Russian Orthodox Christianity, which by now was effectively a tool of the state. The name "Belarusia" ("White Russia"), which had been introduced to replace "Lithuania," was quickly replaced with "Northwestern Territory," and the use of the Belarusian language was banned in schools and publications.

In 1861, the reform-minded Tsar Alexander II abolished serfdom. The emancipated peasants, however, were given too little land for too high a price and subjected to oppressive taxes and corvée; the net result was the impoverishment of farmers, mass migration from the countryside to the cities and abroad, and the encouragement of national-liberal reformers and socialist revolutionaries alike. Economic and cultural discontent in former Poland–Lithuania found expression in a series of patriotic celebrations commemorating historic events from the Commonwealth's past. In Belarus 379 peasant protests were recorded in 1861. In 1862, a group of young middle-class radicals led by

Kastus Kalinouski produced a clandestine anti-Tsarist newspaper, *Muzyckaja Prauda* ("Peasants' Truth"), which championed the peasants, the faithful of the Uniate Church (abolished since 1839), and all who cherished the Belarusian language.

In 1863 there was a pan-national insurrection in former Commonwealth lands against the Tsarist regime. This was swiftly and ruthlessly crushed, and Kalinouski, who had organized the uprising in Belarus and Lithuania, was hanged in Vilnius in 1864. His last letter "from beneath the gallows" has become a political credo of Belarusian nationalism.

Russification was now intensified. The Tsarist government flooded Belarus with teachers, priests, and landlords from Russia, and made the use of the Cyrillic alphabet mandatory for Belarusian.

In the second half of the nineteenth century, the Belarusian economy enjoyed significant growth as the Industrial Revolution spread to Eastern Europe.

Industrialization and urbanization set the stage for the rise of Belarusian self-confidence. A number of authors started publishing in the Belarusian language. Educated Belarusians began to take state office. The Revolution of 1905 resulted in an elected parliament and land reforms, and a surge of national feeling, especially among workers and peasants, gave momentum to the development of a Belarusian literature and press.

Independence and Partition
During the First World War, when Belarus was occupied by Germany, Belarusian culture started to flourish. Schools with Belarusian language, previously banned, were allowed until 1919, when they were banned again by the Polish military administration. Belarus briefly proclaimed independence during the chaos of the Bolshevik revolution —the Belarus National Republic (BNR) was declared on March 25, 1918, in accordance with the terms of the Treaty of Brest-Litovsk. When the Germans withdrew, however, competing national and foreign factions rushed to fill the vacuum. Polish forces invaded

Belarus from the west, and Russians from the east. On January 1, 1919, the Soviet Socialist Republic of Byelorussia was declared in Smolensk. When the Red Army entered Minsk on January 5, 1919, the Rada (Council) of the Belarus National Republic went into exile.

At the end of the Russo–Polish War in 1921, Belarusian territories were divided between Poland and Soviet Russia. The exiled BNR abandoned preparations for a national uprising only when the League of Nations recognized the eastern borders of the Soviet Union on March 15, 1923.

Western Belarus and southern Lithuania were annexed by the Poles, only to be lost in 1939, when they were absorbed into the USSR as part of the Molotov–Ribbentrop Pact. The Polish part of Belarus was subject to Polonization policies, while Soviet Belarus was one of the original republics that formed the USSR.

Stalin's Purges

At first, national culture and language enjoyed a revival in Soviet Belarus. This came to a tragic end

in the 1930s during Stalin's Great Purge against intellectuals and political opponents. The Belarusian writing system was Russified in 1933, and the use of the Belarusian language was discouraged as evidence of an anti-Soviet attitude. Almost all prominent Belarusian intellectuals were executed in the purges. Overall more than 100,000 people were killed and thousands sent to labor camps in Siberia. In 1981 huge numbers of corpses were found at Kurapaty, a wooded area outside Minsk, believed to have been victims of the NKVD (the Soviet secret police). The site now has its own small memorial. Many continued to be persecuted after the war. Despite this, Stalin is still revered by older Belarusians, who refuse to believe that he personally ordered such crimes. On Stalin's death in 1953, people wept openly, never blaming him for what had occurred. Accordingly, little has been done to memorialize his victims, to avoid staining his memory.

The Great Patriotic War
On September 17, 1939, as a result of the secret protocol of the Molotov-Ribbentrop Pact, the Soviet Union invaded Poland and annexed its eastern lands, including most of Polish-held Belarus. When Germany and its allies invaded the Soviet Union on June 22, 1941, the Soviet authorities evacuated about 20 percent of the population of Belarus and destroyed all the food supplies. The country suffered heavily during the fighting. Following bloody encirclement battles, all of Belarus was occupied by the Germans from the end of August 1941 until July 1944.

According to the Nazis' racial "purification" plans, 75 percent of the Belarusian population was to be eliminated. Some 2.2 million people (just over 25 percent of the population) perished during these years. Almost the entire, very large, Jewish population was killed. More than 9,000 villages and one million buildings were destroyed. About 1.1 million Belarusians fought with the Red Army. A further 400,000 became partisans, conducting a nationwide guerrilla campaign against the German forces. Living in dugouts hidden deep in the forests and swamps, they operated across 60 percent of the country,

 disrupting German supply lines and communications, damaging railway tracks, bridges, and telegraph wires, attacking supply depots, fuel dumps, and transports, and ambushing German soldiers. Belarus became known as "the Republic of Partisans." Terrible memories remain close to the surface; particularly brutal are tales of villagers locked in their homes, then burned alive. Thousands met their end in this manner. The horror of war is part of the Belarusian psyche of today, and a subconscious fear of conflict remains, especially among the older generation. Whatever hardships they may endure, they console themselves that modern times are infinitely better than the past.

The Postwar Years
Eighty percent of Minsk was razed during the war, so Stalin had the opportunity to rebuild this frontline "hero city" as his architectural ideal. The building plan combined innovative ideas with

classical architecture, and the surviving prewar buildings and parks were incorporated into the architectural ensemble. The city center was restored in grand neoclassical style, with wide avenues and majestic facades. The main thoroughfare was named Leninsky Avenue (now Nezavisimosti—"Independence") and several imposing squares were built. The oldest part of Minsk is found around the Troitsky suburb, now restored with cobbled alleyways and colorful stucco town houses.

Postwar reconstruction turned Belarus into an industrially, scientifically, and militarily advanced Soviet Republic, enjoying one of the highest living standards within the USSR. This prosperity resulted in a huge immigrant population of Russians in Belarus. Russian became the official language of administration, and the peasant class, the traditional base of the Belarusian nation, ceased to exist.

Perestroika and Independence

From 1986 to 1988, Mikhail Gorbachev, the General Secretary of the Communist Party of the Soviet Union, launched the radical policies of *perestroika* ("restructuring") and *glasnost* ("openness"). These were designed to revitalize the economy, the Communist party, and society. In the new climate, Belarusian intellectuals began to articulate nationalist aspirations; at the same time the Chernobyl disaster alienated increasing numbers of citizens, who realized that information had been knowingly withheld. Details were starting to emerge about the full extent of Stalin's reign of terror. The Belarusian Popular Front (BPF)—a broad cultural movement and political party—was established in 1988 with the aim of attaining democracy and independence through national rebirth. It hoped to encourage reform by actively reducing ties with Russia. However, most people remained attached to Soviet ways and were politically apathetic.

In August 1991, as the Soviet Union broke up, Belarus declared its independence, along with Estonia, Latvia, and Ukraine. In December 1991, Belarus became a founding member of the Commonwealth of Independent States (CIS), an alliance of former Soviet republics (see below, page 42).

The early years of independence were marked by extreme hardship. The centrally controlled Soviet economic system, whereby Belarusian machinery was transported to ready markets throughout the USSR, had disappeared. Many factories now had no buyers for their goods, and the imports Belarusians had been used to receiving also dried up. Rationing and standing in line became part of everyday life.

THE POLITICAL SCENE
Lukashenko Comes to Power

Alexander Grigoryevich Lukashenko, a former collective farm manager, won 80 percent of the popular vote in July 1994, in the last democratic elections to be held to date. As president, he called for a crackdown on crime and corruption, a halt to privatization—including that of land—and renewed economic relations with Russia. By December, two openly critical newspapers had closed down.

Parliament resisted the president's efforts to strengthen his powers. The Constitutional Court overruled a number of presidential decrees, but Lukashenko responded by rewriting the constitution, dissolving parliament, and placing his own appointees on the Constitutional Court. A referendum was held in November 1996, which endorsed the radical new constitution; the Organization for Security and Cooperation in Europe (OSCE) declared it to be "neither free nor fair" and the Constitutional Court ruled it unconstitutional, but Lukashenko pronounced the results binding.

The new constitution gave the president extensive powers; the existing parliament was replaced by a National Assembly with much weaker powers. This consisted of a 110-seat Chamber of Representatives (the lower house) and a 64-seat Council of the Republic (the upper house). Members of the lower house were appointed directly by the president; the upper house consisted of a combination of presidential appointees and winners of the January 1997 elections. The new constitution prolonged Lukashenko's term in office for a further two years to 2001. Western governments refused to recognize the new parliament. Since 1996, many would say that Lukashenko has effectively ruled by decree.

No Apologies

On September 12, 1995, two Americans flying their balloon in an international race were shot down and killed by a Belarusian military helicopter after crossing into Belarusian airspace from Poland. In an official statement, the Belarusian government expressed its regret, but stopped short of an apology, saying that warnings had been given before the balloon was shot down. The race organizers stated that the Belarusian Interior Ministry had been notified of the event in May.

The Repression of Opposing Voices

The first parliamentary elections to be held since the controversial referendum of 1996 took place in 2000. Most opposition parties boycotted them.

Presidential elections took place in 2001, with Lukashenko declaring victory over his two challengers. The OSCE concluded that these elections failed to meet recognized standards, that the state media were biased in favor of Lukashenko, and that opposition candidates had received very limited access to the media.

Parliamentary elections and a referendum held in 2004 to secure support for extending the presidential term were judged "neither free nor fair" by the EU; all the 110 seats contested were won by pro-government candidates. The UK's Minister for Europe commented that "arbitrary use of state power and widespread detentions showed a disregard for the basic rights of freedom of assembly, association and expression, and raise doubts regarding the authorities' willingness to tolerate political competition." It was "an election characterized by intimidation of the electorate, harassment and disruption of the opposition." The constitution was amended once again, removing the two-term presidential limit (Lukashenko was due to leave office in 2006). Opposition figures have declared themselves to be under intense pressure.

Numerous independent media outlets have been suspended or closed, and several journalists have disappeared in mysterious circumstances. While press freedom exists in theory, legislation states that the media cannot slander the president of Belarus or any other government officials, on pain of prosecution.

Black Humor

The head of the central election commission enters the president's study and tells him that she has two pieces of news for him, good and bad. He asks for the good news first.

"You've been reelected president," she declares.

"Okay, and what's the bad news?"

"No one voted for you."

Belarus's presidential elections on March 19, 2006, were accompanied by what many have called wide-scale intimidation. OSCE observers judged it "severely flawed due to the arbitrary use of state power and restrictions on basic rights." The opposition held a number of peaceful protests and set up a tent camp in October Square (emulating that of Ukraine's Orange Revolution). On the evening of March 23, the authorities violently broke up this camp and sealed off the square to prevent further rallies. The demonstrators moved to a nearby park and Alexander Kozulin, a presidential candidate, was arrested after further police action. He was later sentenced to five and a half years' imprisonment. Another leading candidate, Alexander Milinkevich, and three other opposition party leaders were arrested in late April and sentenced to fourteen/fifteen days for "participating in an unauthorized rally"—they had taken part in a demonstration on April 26 to mark the twentieth anniversary of the Chernobyl disaster.

On April 10, 2006, the EU imposed a travel ban on thirty-one individuals, including President Lukashenko, whom they held to be responsible for electoral fraud and civil repression; this was followed by a freezing of personal assets. Four more were added to the list on October 23, 2006, for their prosecution of Kozulin and other opposition activists.

On January 14, 2007, local elections were held. The EU declared them unfair since the opposition was again prevented from campaigning, printing materials, or holding meetings. The Belarus Helsinki Committee reported irregularities and intimidation of opposition candidates and supporters, lack of media equality, and problems with voter lists and counting.

President Lukashenko has voiced his willingness to remain at his post for as long as he is needed. In the meantime, the arrests and detentions continue.

DOMESTIC POLICY

According to UN data, Belarus has one of the highest standards of living, education, and life expectancy within the CIS (men live to sixty-seven on average, women to seventy-seven). It ranked sixty-fourth out of 177 countries worldwide on the UN's Human Development Index in 2007 (compared to Russia in sixty-seventh place, and Ukraine in seventy-sixth). Incomes are low: in early 2008, the average monthly salary was the equivalent of US $351, while purchasing power had halved in comparison with 2001. Many still cannot afford to buy their own homes, and the state has been trying to build more residential housing to ease the situation. Waiting lists for state-owned apartments remain long, obliging many young people to live with their parents for some years.

The state's "socially oriented policy" aims to raise living standards and support a sense of wellbeing. Accordingly, salaries have been steadily, some would say artificially, raised; the president has promised that the average salary will hit US $500 per month within the next few years. Meanwhile, as we have seen, 2006 was declared the Year of the Mother, with a national campaign to encourage families to

have more children. Large families now receive preferential housing terms and child benefits have been increased. Lukashenko called on all women to fulfill their duty by having at least three children, and family life was further supported by making 2007 the Year of the Child, and 2008 the Year of Health. Eighty percent of Belarusians are currently convinced that having a child is a necessity, according to a state survey.

Retirees receive special attention, with pensions rising significantly. Men retire at sixty, women at fifty-five. They form 26.4 percent of the population and are the backbone of the administration's support .

THE ECONOMY

During Soviet times Belarus's industrial base
ensured a relatively high standard of living for the
population. With independence came economic
decline. Industry remains largely under state
control today and is heavily regulated. There is
virtually no private sector/enterprise. Many
production facilities are
out-of-date, inefficient,
and in urgent need of
modernization, by
Western standards.
Belarus has long been
known for its
production of tractors
and dump trucks.

Other major industries are chemical and
petrochemical processing, forestry, and wood
pulp processing, and the production of fertilizers,
radio-electronics, metal-cutting machinery,
televisions, refrigerators, motorcycles, and textiles.
Belarus's main trading partner is Russia, with the
Netherlands, the UK, Ukraine, China, Latvia,
Lithuania, Italy, Poland, and Germany each taking
a small share. The country imports heavily from
Russia (58.1 percent), especially gas and oil.
Meanwhile, Russia accounts for around 37
percent of its total exports. The other CIS
countries take around 9 percent of its exports,
and the EU states about 43 percent.

Belarusian farms—many still modeled on
Soviet "collective" *kolkhoz* lines—produce

potatoes, vegetables, sugar beet, flax, and grain; cattle are bred for beef and dairy products. Agricultural workers remain the lowest-paid group in the country, earning around US $125 a month in 2005, according to the Ministry of Finance. Workers in the oil-processing sector had the highest pay—around US $500, twice the national average. The top earners in the non-production sector were bank employees.

RELATIONS WITH RUSSIA

Close relations with Russia continue to be the main foreign policy priority for Lukashenko. As we have seen, Belarus was a founding member of the CIS in 1991. In January 1995, Russia and Belarus established a Customs Union (later joined by Kazakhstan and Kyrgyzstan). In December 1999, Yeltsin and Lukashenko signed a treaty in Moscow to create a Russian-Belarusian union state. This remains unfulfilled. Some say that the bilateral relationship soured when Vladimir Putin took office. Russia has taken an increasingly assertive line toward all former Soviet states: Putin publicly stated in November 2002 that in the past Russia had given too much to Belarus and that now it was time to take something back. Russia feels that union is desirable in principle, but is demanding economic convergence—entailing significant privatization and liberalization, and an end to lax fiscal and monetary policies. Such conditions are unlikely to be acceptable to Lukashenko as they would undermine his control over the Belarusian economy. Since early 2003, Lukashenko has expressed the desire to see Belarus adopt the Russian ruble as its currency; discussions on this are under way, but terms have not yet been agreed to.

Belarus currently relies on Russia's state-run Gazprom to supply its gas and oil, and derives significant export revenue from their resale. The pipeline running across the country carries Russian gas to Europe. Russia's move to raise energy prices for Belarus has been viewed as "neither friendly nor honest" by Lukashenko. The fear has been voiced that "our manufactures will become more expensive and we won't be able to compete with Russian goods." Since Russia remains Belarus's main trading partner, this is a genuine concern. In return for graduated price increases, Belarus is selling Gazprom 50 percent of the shares in Beltransgas, which runs the pipeline, placing US $2.5 billion in the state coffers over a four-year period.

President Lukashenko has been advocating the building of a nuclear power station to enable Belarus to meet more of its own energy needs. Discussions are ongoing. In addition, he has been courting close relations with Venezuela's Hugo Chavez, signing an accord to jointly exploit gas and oil reserves in this South American country, and generate much-needed revenue.

The public are somewhat bewildered by Russia's aggressive stance, since they have always been led to view their neighbor as a benevolent older brother. People travel freely over the border (no visas are required by Belarusian nationals) and movement between the two capitals is quite common. Everyone seems to have a relative or friend in Moscow. Legislation is in place to ensure equal access to benefits, health care, and education for Russians and Belarusians resident in either state. Those of the older generation often hark back to Soviet days with nostalgia, and voice their support for any policies that bring the two countries closer. Younger people are generally more eager to seek alternatives.

In Soviet times Russian was, naturally, the universal and official language. Following independence in 1991, the Belarusian language underwent a national revival, becoming symbolic of citizens' ability to choose their identity, and was accompanied by the use of a new national flag. By 1996 this flag had been discarded by Lukashenko in favor of an old Soviet-style flag (minus the hammer and sickle). In May 1995, Russian was voted back in as an official national language, on an equal footing with Belarusian. However, Belarusian has been gradually edged out. In 1993, 76 percent of first-year schoolchildren were taught through the medium of Belarusian; by 2006 this figure had dropped to just 18.6 percent. The official equality of these languages seems to apply only to road signs.

RELATIONS WITH THE EU

In response to Belarus's poor performance on constitutional and human rights issues, the EU decided in 1997 to suspend high-level contact. It has promised dialogue and assistance if reform takes place. All aid is suspended, except that used for humanitarian or democratization projects. As we have seen, the 2004 parliamentary elections and referendum were judged "neither free nor fair" by the EU, as was the 2006 presidential election. The EU has frequently called on the Belarusian government to embark on fundamental democratic and economic reform. Travel bans and asset freezes have been imposed in response to the abuse of electoral processes and fundamental human rights.

Of particular concern is the disappearance of four opponents of the regime in 1999–2000, including the former Belarusian Interior Minister Yury Zakharenko. The EU has repeatedly called on the Belarusian authorities to open an independent investigation into this, but they have failed to act. Consequently, in September 2004, the EU applied travel restrictions against those Belarusian officials thought to be involved. In response to the state's move to widen its powers of arrest in late 2005, the EU called on the Belarusian National Assembly to reconsider. These calls were ignored. In May 2007, the United Nations General

Assembly rejected a bid by Belarus to join its Human Rights Council. In addition, Belarus's observer status on the Council of Europe was suspended in November 2007.

Parts of Europe rely on Belarus to pump the gas they need from Russia. In addition, their processed oil imports often come directly from Belarus.

RELATIONS WITH THE REST OF THE WORLD

On December 8, 1991, the heads of eleven sovereign states (Armenia, Azerbaijan, Belarus, Kazakhstan, Kyrgyzstan, Moldova, Russia, Tajikistan, Turkmenistan, Uzbekistan, and Ukraine) gathered at the government residence in the village of Viskuly in Belarus's Belovezhskaya Pushcha nature reserve, and signed a protocol to establish the CIS. Georgia joined in 1993. Within this organization, member states are supposed to enjoy preferential trade and mutual support. The headquarters are in Minsk.

The Belarusian leadership has been cultivating political and trade relations with Venezuela, China, Iran, North Korea, and Cuba.

In February 1993, Belarus acceded to the Nuclear Non-proliferation Treaty and ratified the Strategic Arms Reduction Treaty (START I). In 1996, it fulfilled its undertaking to become a nuclear-free state. Tactical nuclear warheads were withdrawn from the country in 1992, and the last strategic missiles left Belarus for Russia in 1996

(a decision that Lukashenko has subsequently called "regrettable"). In 1995, Belarus signed NATO's Partnership for Peace Agreement. However, Lukashenko is a critic of NATO enlargement. He believes that nonintervention in other states' affairs is appropriate. NATO indicated that his presence at its summit in Prague in November 2002 would be unwelcome, and the Czechs subsequently refused him a visa.

According to state statistics, almost 3.5 million Belarusians (more than a third of the resident population) live outside the Republic of Belarus—two million in former Soviet republics. Increasing numbers are thought to be emigrating to Europe, the USA, and Canada.

chapter two

VALUES &
ATTITUDES

THE BELARUSIAN CHARACTER
Sociability and Culture
Belarusians are enormously sociable, and have a
huge capacity for enjoyment. They need little
persuasion to party, and view holidays as occasions
for plenty of singing and dancing. They adore
music, particularly traditional folk songs, and the
highlight of the year is the Slavonic Bazaar, a song
contest held in Vitebsk. Singing and dancing are
prominent in the school curriculum, and public
performances are common.

Belarusians also believe that a well-rounded
person should have an appreciation of culture.
Literature, art, ballet, and opera are heavily state
subsidized, ensuring that performances and
exhibitions are well attended. Young people take
part in cultural activities, with many belonging to
musical or dance groups. Meanwhile, most older
women sew their own clothes, embroider, and
knit. Each town has its own Palace of Culture
where traditional crafts are encouraged alongside
contemporary art forms.

LITERARY HEROES

In the early twentieth century, "Belorussian" was associated dismissively with folklore, peasant ways, and ethnic customs. The Belarusian poets Yanka Kupala and Yakub Kolas countered this by writing inspirational works on rural themes in order to encourage national pride.

Yanka Kupala, the pen name of Ivan Dominikovich Lucevich (1882–1942), is the foremost poet and playwright—often called the "National Prophet"—of Belarus. Most of his works were banned from the 1930s onward because of their  ardent patriotism. He fought to preserve the dying Belarusian language during the Soviet Russification policy, and his death in Moscow in 1942 of unknown causes is speculated to have been murder by the regime.

Yakub Kolas, the pen name of Kanstancin Miskievich (1882–1956), is the next well-known Belarusian literary figure. He, too, opposed the Tsarist regime and was imprisoned for three years for activism. His early works describe the suffering of the peasantry, while his poem "The  Fisherman's Hut" (1947) tells of Belarus's struggle after unification with the Soviet state. Today many institutions and streets in Belarus bear their names.

A love of classical literature, music, and dance, particularly venerating the grand masters of Russia (Rachmaninoff, Shostakovich, Gogol, Pushkin, Dostoevsky, Tchaikovsky, and Chekov) is a must for Belarusians, and, of course, they have their own poets, such as Yakub Kolas and Yanka Kupala. Friendly soirées often see the Belarusians reciting poetry and pulling guests into joining hearty renditions of well-known folk songs.

Friends and Neighbors
Belarusians most enjoy entertaining friends; they'll sit in the kitchen for hours putting the world to rights. Success in life can largely be measured by the strength of friendships and family bonds. People are often very close to their neighbors, looking out for one another with a strong sense of social responsibility. They'll keep in touch with school companions throughout their entire lives. It is for this that you'll come to love Belarusians. They are sincere, warmhearted, good-humored, and thoughtful.

Endurance
The hardships of the past decades have taught Belarusians resilience and resourcefulness. The women are particularly strong, often coming home from a full day's work to cook, clean, wash, iron, and look after children. They are remarkably hardworking. In contrast, the men can appear less industrious and, during tough times, are more likely to become depressed or resort to alcohol.

Stoicism in the face of hardship is typical, but this can tip over into fatalism in the older generation, who are inured to suffering; they believe trials are sent to be endured.

Sports
Sports are also encouraged: cross-country skiing and ice hockey are among the most televised, and young people are strongly encouraged to join teams. Tennis and soccer are also currently enjoying great popularity.

ATTITUDES TO THE COUNTRYSIDE

In pre-Soviet times, Belarus was largely agrarian. In the mid-twentieth century it became industrialized and supplied machinery to the rest of the USSR. By 1991, it was the richest CIS state. This created a divide between town and country people. The urbanites are better educated, with greater access to the theater and museums, and have higher incomes. They tend to view village life as provincial and old-fashioned and feel intellectually superior to their country cousins. However, even the most sophisticated Minsk dwellers have a special place in their hearts for the countryside. Summer weekends are often spent at the country *dacha* (a simple wooden home) or with village relatives, enjoying forest walks, fishing, and mushroom picking. Connections with country life are cherished.

Older country folk are content to enjoy their traditional ways and are rarely tempted to visit the city, but young people are moving to towns in ever increasing numbers, lured by the bright lights and greater employment opportunities.

ATTITUDES TO WORK

Most Belarusians want a simple job without responsibility or burden; in many jobs, opportunities for advancement are limited anyway, especially for women. Those working for state-run enterprises have little incentive to work hard or be innovative, since they are generally paid the same monthly wage regardless of their efforts. At harvest time, those who have brought in the crops most efficiently might receive a small cash bonus. A similar scheme is adopted in some factories, where an "achievement wall" displays photos of hardworking staff.

The Work Ethic

Old Soviet Era adage: "We pretend to work, and they pretend to pay us."

An office worker walks in and catches his colleague gazing out of the window one morning. "What are you doing?" he reproaches him. "You shouldn't be looking out of the window at this time of the day. If you start doing that now, how will you fill up the afternoon?"

However, in recent years, the entrepreneurial spirit has been developing. Minsk has thousands of small market traders (at the outdoor markets, in underpasses, and inside the larger stores like GUM and TSUM) and small and medium-sized businesses are beginning to grow in number.

COMMUNAL SPIRIT

For centuries, villages were largely self-governing small communities where life centered on farming. People's interests were bound together by the common need for a good harvest, and their identity was shaped by membership in the group. It was unthinkable to be solitary.

The Soviets were able to exploit this social order, turning these traditional farming communities into agricultural collectives, or *kolkhoz*. People were encouraged to see themselves as part of a much larger entity. Taking an interest in other people's affairs wasn't just friendly; it was a sign that you had the correct "soviet" mentality. (*soviet* means "advice" in Russian). At its best, this meant caring for your neighbors in times of trouble; at its worst, it took the form of informing on them to save yourself.

Although people are now less intrusive of their neighbors' business than they once were, a feeling of communal responsibility remains. Accordingly, even in Minsk, strangers may stop to tell someone that they are behaving badly. Older women may remind you to button up your coat or put on your hat, scarf, and gloves. If you have any kind of ailment, advice will be forthcoming on remedies you should try. Don't be irritated or offended—people are showing that they care about you.

Inevitably, however, times are beginning to change. Parents are now eager for their children to outshine their peers and push them aggressively through school and university; study is essential to secure a well-paid job (especially in IT). The realities of "me first" are hitting home, and the new generations don't want to be left behind.

ATTITUDES TO AUTHORITY

Belarusians' lives were tightly controlled by the state in Soviet times. They placed their trust in higher powers and never thought to question them. A notable exception occurred in the wake of the Chernobyl disaster, when information regarding the seriousness of the accident was withheld for weeks, while children played outdoors exposed to radiation. Although people were eventually moved away from the worst affected areas, thousands still live in mildly radioactive environments. Unsurprisingly, even today many have little faith in public information, such as radiation safety labels on food products.

Belarus is now an independent republic, but it is governed in a similar style to that of Soviet times, with the president closely overseeing all his ministers' work and ideology being taught in the school curriculum. People largely accept decisions from above and rarely express contrary opinions.

WOMEN IN SOCIETY

Traditionally, peasant women worked in the fields, ran the home, and raised the children, while men headed the household and saw to the running of communal farms. Girls from upper-class families had greater access to education, but

it was only in the late nineteenth century that some middle-class women, after studying at universities in Vilnius, St. Petersburg, and Moscow, began to enter the professions. Medicine, law, and teaching were the most common choices. The year 1917 was a turning point, since women finally gained the vote, opening up new horizons.

The Soviet state declared equal voting and socioeconomic rights for men and women; of course, the reality was that women were expected to work full-time while also looking after their household. In 1930s Belarus, 40 percent of all skilled workers were female, with thousands moving to cities from villages. Many also worked on building sites, mastering such skills as bricklaying and plumbing. Today, women serve in the army and police force and are well represented proportionally in higher education.

In modern day Belarus, motherhood is the ultimate status symbol. Most young women marry their childhood sweethearts, but there are certainly some who set out to find themselves an eligible bachelor, usually older than themselves and with a healthy bank account. Any foreign man visiting Belarus should expect to be approached by (or introduced to) young women who will see him in this light. Despite marrying young and often having their first child in their twenties, well-educated women also commonly pursue careers. Those with fewer qualifications

 generally work on farms or in low-paid manual jobs such as factory work or cleaning.

Gender equality in the workplace has some way to go. Women are certainly underrepresented in top levels of management and in government. They are usually paid less for the same work, and employers can be reluctant to hire them, assuming they'll take off too much time to have or care for children.

There is no legislation directly governing sexual harassment. Most Belarusians, like many other Europeans, consider office flirtations to be the norm. In fact, women expect a certain amount of attention and compliments, and like to be treated in an "old-fashioned" chivalrous fashion: they expect men to help them with their coats, open doors and pull out chairs for them, and, often, pay for meals and drinks.

Belarusian women strike foreigners as being well-groomed, stylishly dressed (albeit rather provocatively), and generally very attractive. Most are tall and slim, though in later years they tend to put on weight, becoming the *babushkas* of popular legend. Most are well-mannered, well-educated, and independent. They don't

tend to get tipsy and misbehave themselves, or use vulgar language. They are worthy of admiration.

The issue of human trafficking has recently come into focus in Belarus. Many vulnerable young women who are tempted to seek "better" lives abroad may find themselves sold as sex slaves, having been lured by the promise of a husband, a good job, or a modeling career. To a lesser extent, trafficking also touches the lives of Belarusian men, who travel abroad seeking work on construction sites, often in Russia; they may find themselves trapped, working for little more than a roof over their head and their meals.

In a bid to protect Belarusian women from being exploited, education programs are being set up at schools and universities to inform them of the dangers of traveling abroad with strangers. Border guards are also being trained to spot suspicious activities, and victim support groups exist to help those women fortunate enough to return to their families.

THE GENERATION GAP

One of the first things you'll notice in Belarus is that there is a huge divide between the younger and older generations. Younger people are keen to travel and are open to ideas from the West. They take great pride in their appearance and spend a large proportion of their income on clothes and going out. Some may think the easiest answer to their problems is to emigrate, but most are patriotically attached to their native land and want to improve life in Belarus. They are bursting with energy, but the political climate obliges them to be discreet about voicing their opinions in front of strangers. Significant numbers are also sympathetic toward the opposition party but are understandably wary of openly attending rallies or taking part in campaigning. Increasingly, younger people are eager to ensure a good standard of living for themselves, and are ready to work hard to achieve their goals.

Those who grew up in the early postwar years are more fatalistic. Under Soviet rule, they had little control over their own lives and endured years of hardship, yet there were certain welcome certainties, such as cheap food and utilities. Generally, they are grateful to the president for bringing stability from the chaotic early years of independence. From their late forties onward, people often appear much older than they really are, perhaps worn out by a life of worry. They are hugely resilient, but tend to accept whatever fate throws at them rather than struggling to achieve change. Those aged seventy and beyond are the president's backbone of supporters; they recall the war years and are simply grateful for a roof over their heads and a meager pension.

ATTITUDES TO MONEY

One of the most refreshing aspects of life in Belarus is the lack of materialism. Of course, people like to have a comfortable home, a car that works, a warm coat, and so on, but consumerism doesn't exist on anywhere near the same scale as in America or most of Europe. The idea of shopping as a leisure activity is almost unknown. Quite simply, people don't have huge amounts of disposable income; nor is there much in the shops to tempt them. Spending time with friends—usually just walking together or chatting at home—is most people's idea of the perfect weekend. Throw in a concert or a trip to an ice-hockey match and they are in heaven.

Many Belarusians are obliged to spend a large part of their income on daily necessities: rent, utilities, and food. Even though all these things are subsidized by the state, they remain relatively expensive, particularly in Minsk. For most people, a night out is a rare treat. Of course, younger people, living with their parents and free of much financial responsibility, are more likely to spend time in cafés and buy cosmetics, new clothes, and other "treats." You may notice, however, that many will nurse a single cup of coffee for almost an hour or will just order an inexpensive salad or soup from the menu. When a man takes a girl out, she will certainly expect him to pay the bill.

Minsk's elite clearly enjoy a very different lifestyle—shopping at the few designer stores, driving luxury cars, and gambling in casinos. These people are treated warily by most Belarusians. If you amass large sums of money here, people tend to be a little suspicious about how you did it.

Corruption

Although President Lukashenko came to power on the strength of his stand against corruption, and has passed much legislation to curb official abuse, most businessmen still find themselves obliged to pay the occasional bribe to navigate low-level bureaucracy. International Finance Corporation reports have shown that most small- and medium-sized businesses (that is, privately

 run rather than state-owned) are commonly obliged to pay bribes in order to obtain the permits and licenses they need to operate. In 2007, Transparency International ranked Belarus 150th out of 179 countries,

with Russia in 143rd place. Ordinary people tend to underreport their income (to avoid taxes) and are not above helping friends with small bureaucratic matters; they do not view such behavior as criminal.

Most teenagers with fair academic abilities are given the opportunity of further education, but Belarusians are fully aware that nepotism remains in state-run organizations and enterprises, with jobs being found for friends and relatives.

ATTITUDES TO RUSSIANS

On the whole, Belarusians see Russians as kindred spirits. Most people have relatives or friends living in Russia, and many take trips there on a regular basis. No visa is required, and there is an excellent rail system connecting the major cities to those of their neighbor. Moreover, during Soviet times, Belarusians were encouraged to see themselves as Russians. This attitude is still promoted in independent Belarus, with Russia portrayed as a supportive elder brother. Culturally, the two countries share much and, undoubtedly, Belarus relies heavily on trade with Russia.

Belarusians do, however, feel themselves to have a separate identity, especially those born from the 1970s onward; concerts and exhibitions celebrating traditional Belarusian folk music, dancing, and crafts are very popular, as are contemporary displays of modern Belarusian arts.

Many people approve of the idea of forming a "Union State" with Russia, possibly because they cannot imagine existing without Russian economic support; the opposition parties, largely supported by young Belarusians, are vocal in opposing it. Faith in Russia was shaken by the Gazprom situation, whereby prices for oil and gas were dramatically raised after years of subsidy.

Minskers traveling to Moscow often return lamenting how dirty, congested, and expensive the city has become. In their minds, there is no contest between the two. Moscow's power and wealth (albeit rather unevenly distributed) is unquestioned but Belarusians have an enduring love for their own cities. They see themselves as more honest, friendly, and in touch with nature. Perversely, this is just how villagers see themselves in comparison to Belarusian urbanites. Muscovites tend to view Minskers as little more than provincial peasants.

ATTITUDES TO FOREIGNERS

Most Belarusians have little experience of foreigners. During Soviet times, few outsiders visited, and even since 1991 Belarus has remained relatively insular; the granting of a visa cannot be taken for granted. Most foreigners are businessmen or members of official organizations such as embassies or the UN, and are usually only encountered in Minsk and the larger cities.

Older people generally speak little English. Even young people, who have studied it at school, often lack the confidence to speak, their lessons having revolved around written translations rather than speaking skills. Belarus is far from being cosmopolitan; an Asian or dark-skinned face still attracts a lot of attention, although, as the universities take on more students from China and Korea, this may change. Interracial marriages are almost unheard of, although Belarusians are far too polite to show any prejudice.

Small numbers of tourists do visit Belarus but, even so, most ordinary people may never have met a foreigner face-to-face, let alone spoken to one. As the local media portrays the West in a largely negative light, they are understandably mistrustful of the idea of foreigners. Nevertheless, on meeting you, their reaction will likely be one of curiosity, soon followed by warmth.

Depending on their political allegiance, Belarusians view Europeans and Americans as representatives of states who are either trying to help Belarus or trying to interfere. Politics is a touchy subject; even those who are open and friendly are likely to be wary of discussing their views. The Soviet legacy of feeling that you are being watched remains; indeed, as a foreigner, you may have your rooms bugged by the Belarusian KGB. Your Belarusian hosts will be polite from the outset, although rather formal. Once they know you a little better, you'll see their warmer side. If you truly hit it off, you'll have friends for life.

ATTITUDES TO HOMOSEXUALITY
In Soviet times, homosexual acts were punishable by a five-year prison sentence. This was revoked in Belarus in 1992, but homosexuality remains largely frowned upon as unnatural. Many people deny it exists, saying it's an outside "corruption."

There is no visible "gay scene." Ideas are very old-fashioned; even your most liberal-minded Belarusian friends may have strong feelings on this issue. Although homosexuals are not barred from the armed forces, the first deputy chief of the Defense Ministry's Main Ideological Directorate has publicly stated that "those with such sexual orientation prefer to go abroad . . . there are no such problems here."

ATTITUDES TO MINORITIES

Just over 80 percent of the population are native Belarusian. Around 11 percent are Russian; many were settled here after the war to bolster the workforce. Poles make up 3.9 percent and Ukrainians 2.4 percent. Other nationalities make up a further 1.1 percent (1999 census). This category consists mainly of citizens of other CIS states. If you see people of other nationalities on the streets of Minsk—say, Germans, Americans, or British—they are most likely to be diplomats or members of international organizations such as the UN or OSCE. Some may be visiting businessmen, or people working for Chernobyl charities. Few are simply tourists. The universities accept some foreign students, particularly from China, and some from West Africa.

Around 80 percent of Belarusians describe themselves as Eastern Orthodox, and most of the rest are Roman Catholic. Protestants, Jews, and Muslims are very much in the minority, but generally people are tolerant of their presence. Evangelical missions, however, have had difficulty establishing themselves, since the authorities often perceive them as unwelcome "cults."

Belarus, we have seen, first became Christian in 992 CE. In time, religious and national identity became entwined as the native Autocephalous Orthodox Church, the rival Roman Catholic Church, the attempted compromise of the Uniate Church, and the imperial Russian Orthodox Church vied for control. All religion was suppressed by the Soviet regime and went underground. Today many people have returned to the churches, which are being beautifully restored and adorned with new icons. Here, the Belarusian love of art and music is complemented by the comfort they gain from shared experiences. The devout attend Sunday mass regularly. Even non-observant Belarusians have a natural spirituality that is evident in all aspects of their lives: they have a mystical streak, are apt to believe in ancient superstitions, have a great reverence for the beauty of their land, and believe we should "do as we would be done by." The Belarusians are bighearted and life-embracing people, albeit small-minded on occasion.

Belarus was home to 10 percent of the world's Jewish population before the Second World War. As in most Nazi occupied countries, Jews were rounded up into ghettos before being transported to concentration camps and killed. Around 800,000 are thought to have died. Descendants of relatives sometimes travel to Belarus to trace their family roots and visit Jewish cemeteries and massacre sites.

SUPERSTITIONS

Old pagan traditions remain strongly ingrained. A few of the most widely held beliefs follow.

Mirrors are thought to have strange powers. Each time you look in a mirror it supposedly takes a small part of your life force, and the longer you own one the more powerful it becomes. If you break a mirror, this isn't bad luck in itself, but all its energy will fly away, and it needs to replace this. So, don't look into a broken mirror, or it will sap your life force. If you should leave the house, and have to return unexpectedly for something you have forgotten, you must look in the mirror as soon as you enter and change something about your appearance, to avoid bad luck. Mirrors are covered when a household member has died; their spirit is thought to linger for forty days and may be sighted in any uncovered reflective surface. Not surprisingly, it's considered dangerous for a newborn baby to look in a mirror.

Don't whistle indoors; the sound is thought to fly out of the window, carrying everyone's financial good luck with it. Also, it is believed that all financial debts should be paid before New Year's Eve; otherwise a year of debt lies ahead.

Table etiquette has a host of superstitions. Singletons should never sit at a corner, unless they want to remain unmarried. If someone drops a fork or spoon, a female guest will soon appear; a fallen knife heralds a male. To reverse this, tap the utensil on the table three times and say, "Stay at home." Playing with your knife is bad form, and is supposed to encourage arguments. If there are thirteen people at the table, two must be in love, even if they don't know it; this gives plenty of scope for teasing. Once a bottle is empty it should be speedily removed, otherwise there will be no full bottles in future. Sitting between two people of the same name is very lucky.

Belarus is well-known for its *ruchniks*—narrow cloths embroidered in red on white—which have long been thought to have protective qualities, rather like amulets against evil. Peasants would embroider their hemlines, cuffs, and collars in symbolic patterns to ward off the attentions of any mischievous demons. During the Great Patriotic War, men were sent away wearing their *ruchniks* close to their hearts, in the hope that these would ensure their safe return. The *ruchnik* was originally worn as a belt, but now can also be a simple cloth (sometimes used to cover bread) or headscarf.

Before leaving home, it is customary to sit silently beside your suitcase for a minute; this gives your spirit time to rejoin your body from wherever it is residing in the house, ensuring you depart in full vigor.

chapter three

FESTIVALS & CUSTOMS

STATE HOLIDAYS

The Belarusians eagerly look forward to their official holidays, many of which are accompanied by state-organized outdoor concerts and fireworks displays. New Year is undoubtedly the best-loved holiday, although it's also quite private, with most celebrations taking place at home. The biggest public event is Victory Day, when parades and concerts fill the city streets and parks.

January 1: New Year's Day
January 7: Orthodox Christmas
March 8: Women's Day
March 15: Constitution Day
Ninth day after Easter: Radunitsa (Orthodox Remembrance Day, for ancestors)
May 1: Workers' Day
May 9: Victory Day
July 3: Independence Day
December 25: Christmas Day

The state holidays are a mixture of old Soviet celebrations and revived Orthodox festivities. They are official days off work, although many shops, cafés, and restaurants stay open.

New Year's Day
In Soviet times, people were forbidden to practice their religious beliefs. To keep the tradition of a midwinter festival, New Year was elevated to the status of everyone's favorite holiday. In fact, it is on New Year's Eve that families gather together to celebrate the passing of the old year and welcome in the new. It's said that the way you spend this evening will determine your fortune in the year ahead, so people like to surround themselves with their family or friends and serve quantities of tasty food. Most spend all night partying and even the youngest children are allowed to stay up with their parents, since gifts are exchanged after midnight. In modern day Minsk, many young people set off to promenade through the streets around 1:00 a.m.

Peter the Great brought Christmas trees to Russia in the eighteenth century, having seen them in Europe. A decorated *yolka* (fir tree) became a well-loved symbol of the festival. It was one of the hardest things for people to put aside, so Stalin reintroduced it as a New Year Tree. All over modern Belarus, huge, elaborately illuminated trees are placed prominently in city squares, often with ice rinks picturesquely created around them.

St. Nicholas's Feast Day (December 6) was observed in Russia for centuries. As a Christian figure, St. Nicholas was reinvented as Ded Moroz (Grandfather Frost) under the Soviets. He wears a long red coat, a fur hat, and white felt boots (*valenki*), and has a white beard. In an effort to make him appear less like his Western counterpart, he

sometimes appears in blue. He carries a magic staff and his sleigh is pulled by three horses (a *troika*). He is helped by his beautiful granddaughter, Snegurochka (the Snow Maiden).

Rather confusingly, one legend surrounding her says that a childless couple made her from snow and she came to life, only to melt when spring came. She magically reappears each winter. Children are just as likely to make a snow maiden as a snowman. Grandfather Frost often comes to visit children in the days leading up to New Year (in children's clubs or in restaurants), to check on how they are behaving themselves. He asks them to recite poems about winter, and Snegurochka may hand out sweets. On New Year's Eve itself, he comes, once the children are asleep, to leave their gifts.

Christmas

Despite being forbidden for so many years, Belarusians have returned with verve, since independence in 1991, to their traditional Christian festivals. Russian Orthodox believers still follow the old Julian calendar, celebrating Christmas on January 7, while Catholics and Protestants observe the Gregorian calendar date of December 25. Both are recognized as state holidays. These dates are quiet affairs when compared to New Year, however.

Their pagan roots lie in the winter solstice festival of Kaliady, celebrated from December 25 to January 7, which marked the turning of the year. Some Belarusians keep the traditions alive, dressing up as animals and parading through their villages at this time. A sun and a toy goat's head are carried (representing fertility) and carolers visit each house hoping for edible treats. The family traditionally partakes of *kasha* (porridge), made from barley, and served with honey, poppy seeds, nuts, and raisins; the master of the house takes the first spoonful and a plate is left outside to appease Zuzia, the god of winter. This was always a time for fortune-telling, and families still indulge in lighthearted antics such as drawing straws to see who will live the longest. Various rituals identify future husbands and discover who will be the first to marry. Festivities effectively start on December 25 and continue right through to mid-January, so this is a period to avoid if you are planning business meetings.

Women's Day

Women's Day was another major holiday on the Soviet calendar (adopted shortly after the 1917 October Revolution) and remains an occasion to praise women for their hard work throughout the year. It's a florists' favorite, with prices rising significantly, as a man who goes home without flowers and chocolates will not be forgiven. Wives, mothers, sisters, and girlfriends all expect a little something from the men in their lives. Women also give each other small gifts. Restaurants are booked up weeks in advance, so beware. This is far more popular than the newly arrived Valentine's Day, and is truly an occasion for women to receive the praise they are due. There are also special TV programs and concerts to honor wives and mothers.

Constitution Day

This celebrates the day in 1994 when Belarus set up its present-day constitution. A relatively new holiday, it doesn't arouse the same emotional response as many of the others.

Radunitsa (Remembrance Day)

On the ninth day after Orthodox Easter, believers remember deceased relatives. Its name comes from the verb *radovatsia*, "to be glad." The idea is to share the joy of Easter with deceased family members by visiting their graves with flowers,

Easter eggs, and cakes, which
are left for the departed
spirits. Graves are also
covered with protective
ruchniks, which have special
significance within the
family. Celebrations also
occur at several other times
during the year, depending
on the region. Radunitsa is

essentially a Russian Orthodox festival, while All
Souls' (November 2) is the Roman Catholic
equivalent. However, the origins are in pagan
Dzyady celebrations, when families gathered at
the graves, pouring a libation of vodka and
leaving *kasha,* pancakes, meat, and fried eggs.

Workers' Day
This public holiday is marked by concerts and
public entertainments in parks around the
country. It's a popular day for picnics and *shashlyk*
barbecues.

Victory Day
This commemorates victory in the Second World
War (known as the Great Patriotic War). Huge
celebrations are held around the country, and
Minsk hosts the central event: a march of veterans
wearing uniforms and medals. Every family lost
relatives in the war (25 percent of the population
died in those years) so this occasion has solemn
significance for Belarusian citizens. Films and

documentaries on the war
years are often shown on
Belarusian TV, but there are
more around this time. The
parade includes a patriotic

celebration of all things Belarusian, from
refrigerators, tractors, and bags of cement to young
people cavorting in gymnastic routines and
national teams displaying their talents en route
(recently including mobile boxing rings and tennis
courts). Later, October Square and the parks
resound with concerts, dancing, and people having
fun, and around 10:00 p.m. a huge firework display
illuminates the city.

Independence Day
This celebration marks the anniversary of the
1944 liberation of Minsk by the Soviet Red Army
in the Second World War, not Belarusian
independence from the USSR. Some Belarusians
mark March 25 as a national Independence Day.
This date is not a public holiday and has, in fact,
become closely associated with the opposition,
who try to organize rallies around this time. In
1918 on this date, the first Belarusian Democratic
Republic was created, lasting very briefly until
subsumed by Russia.

OTHER FESTIVALS
Defenders' Day (formerly Red Army Day)
Although not a public holiday, this celebration,

dating from Soviet times, has great importance. An official ceremony is held in Victory Square and wreaths are laid at all war memorials. Every Belarusian man has to serve eighteen months' military conscription so, in fact, February 23 has become a day for women to praise all men. Husbands are cosseted, and in the workplace men enjoy some attention and little treats from their female colleagues.

Maslenitsa: Pancake Week (start of Lent)
Westerners have one day, but the Belarusians a whole week of pancake (or *blini*) eating. The pagan roots of the festival (welcoming the sun) are far more evident here than in Western Europe. Traditionally, a man is chosen to dress as Lady Maslenitsa ("Lady Butter"), and is paraded amidst revelry to encourage abundance in the year ahead. On the final day, Forgiveness Sunday, bonfires are lit and a large straw doll of Lady Maslenitsa is burned to say farewell to winter. In Minsk, this traditionally happens in the square near the Palace of Sport. Expect to find public entertainment in the parks and plenty of people with open braziers for outdoor pancake cooking. Served variously with garlic, mushrooms, sour cream, caviar, or jam, they are wonderfully tasty.

Easter
Again, the Christian aspects of Easter are blended with ancient Belarusian customs. Easter cakes, *koulitch*, are popular, alongside *paskha* puddings,

made with raisins, sour milk, and eggs. Coloring eggs is a common pastime with children, particularly in onion water to make them turn an ochre color. Washing your face in the leftover water is said to ensure good health and beauty for the rest of the year.

Kupalle

This pagan celebration of fertility is one of the most joyful and enduring. It celebrates the summer solstice, the longest day of the year. On Kupalle night, the trees in the forests are said to walk and speak, while supernatural creatures wander the earth searching for mischief. Many legends surround this special date but one of the best-known is that of the flowering fern, said to bloom once a year only on this night, with a glowing crimson flower. Anyone finding it will miraculously comprehend the language of plants and animals until the sun rises and, more importantly, will be able to use the flower to see beneath the earth, making it the perfect tool for discovering buried treasure. In rural areas, the festival is widely celebrated. Girls make garlands for their hair that may be thrown into flowing water for a spot of fortune-telling—if yours sinks, you'll marry the following year. The most common activity is fire jumping. Couples can jump over together hand-in-hand, but if their hands part it foretells the end of their love. Water is also said to have amazing properties on Kupalle night. It's said that mystic forces illuminate rivers and lakes from midnight until dawn; a nighttime dip brings youth and vitality. The more reserved make do with a roll in the dew. The church later adopted the date as St. John's Day, to give it some semblance of propriety.

WEDDINGS

Although 68 percent of marriages in Belarus end in divorce, this isn't deterring young people from tying the knot. The average age for women to marry is an innocent twenty-two, and for men twenty-four. Those wishing to marry don't bother with being "engaged" in the sense the West knows it, and there's no engagement ring. Instead, they apply to a state register office. After a one-month "cooling off" period, the couple can return to complete the legal paperwork and emerge as husband and wife. This official ceremony is usually performed very quietly. Soon after, however, most couples have a big church service, which is viewed as the real wedding. The groom goes to collect his bride from her home, and is intercepted by her friends as he arrives. Before being allowed to take his beloved away, he is obliged to fulfill challenges to prove himself worthy of her, such as identifying her from a selection of baby photos.

During the service, a Russian Orthodox tradition is for the couple to race to a ceremonial carpet, called in Belarus the *padnozhnik*. The first to step on to it will wear the trousers in the relationship. On leaving the church, the wedding party takes a tour of the local memorials. They lay flowers to recognize their debt to those who laid down their lives, and have photos taken. In Minsk, the most popular spots are beside the eternal flame in Victory Square, in Gorky Park, and on the Isle of Tears in the River Svislach (the Afghan memorial).

At the reception, the newlyweds are met by their parents bearing salt and a *karavai* (a round loaf of bread), symbolizing prosperity in their future home. They fight one another to see who can bite or tear off the biggest chunk, again to determine supremacy in the marriage. On a more solemn note, they have their hands tied with a *ruchnik*, showing that they are bound to one another. A traditional joke is to encourage the couple to kiss by declaring the champagne bitter (*gor'ko*). The couple must turn it sweet by kissing for as long as possible. The *tamada* (toastmaster) has a huge role to play in encouraging high jinks and jokes at the pair's expense; the success or failure of the wedding day is often laid at his door. Many families observe the Georgian tradition of "kidnapping" the bride, whereby she is whisked off and only returned once the guests have donated an appropriate ransom.

FUNERALS

A person's soul is thought to linger in the home for forty days. Accordingly, food and drink are left out for them during this time—usually honey, water, and vodka. Mirrors are covered, since it's thought that spirits may be seen in the reflective surface. The funeral is the one occasion when vodka toasts are not made to the "guest of honor," flowers are always brought in even numbers, and it's traditional to kiss the deceased on the forehead. On the final day, the doors and windows are left open so that the soul can escape easily. In days gone by, the embroidered *ruchnik* cloth belonging to the deceased was hung at the window, to help the soul find its path the next world. The *ruchnik* was then buried with its owner.

chapter four

MAKING FRIENDS

It's easy to become friendly with Belarusians, but, as an outsider, it's unlikely that you will ever attain the status of a close friend. Such bonds are forged in the formative teenage years, especially at university, but can date from early childhood. Annual school reunions are a major event in many people's social calendars, with such friendships sustained for an entire lifetime. Close friends are small in number and are expected to be available day or night in times of need; as such, they are highly valued. Family bonds are vital, with people relying heavily on their cousins, siblings, and parents for practical help and advice, but "soul mates" are just as important.

If you are coming to Belarus to work, you'll have an automatic entrance into friendships. Taking a job teaching English at one of the language schools is a perfect way to meet people, with students and teachers likely to suggest going for coffee after hours. They'll be keen to gain extra practice and will quiz you on life back home. Likewise, if you are taking part in charity work, your local contacts will be eager to get to know you better. If you are just passing through, it will be much harder; striking up a conversation at an art gallery, sports event, or bar isn't easy when people have a limited command of English. If you can speak Russian, you may have more success, but avoid being pushy.

NAMES AND INTRODUCTIONS

In line with their Russian neighbors, Belarusians have three names: their first name, their patronymic (taken from their father's name), and their surname. You'll usually be told the first two, for example Igor Ivanovich (Igor, son of Ivan) or Olga Ivanovna (Olga, daughter of Ivan). This is very formal and polite. It's good to address your acquaintance by both names, if you can remember them. They may then ask you to be more familiar and just call them by their first name. As a non-Russian / non-Belarusian, you aren't expected to use a patronymic yourself.

In addition, most first names have a diminutive (an affectionate shortened version). You'll no doubt hear these being used and may be invited to use them too. It's polite to wait until this is suggested. Valentin may be Valeg, Alexander is often Sasha, and Mikhail is Misha. Tatiana is Tanya, Ludmilla is Luda, Victoria is Vikar, and Anastacia may be Anya. In many offices there is more than one Alexander, in which case the older one will be Big Sasha, and the younger Little Sasha. Close friends commonly make diminutives by adding —*ka* to a name (meaning "little one," hence, "beloved"). Irina becomes Irinka, and Lena Lenochka. The —*ka* can be added to lots of other Russian words (potatoes are *kartoshka* and bread rolls are *bouloshka*); this reveals the affectionate attitude toward basic foodstuffs.

If you are unfamiliar with the Russian language, you may be unaware that there are two forms of address: *vy* and *ty* (like the French *vous* and *tu*). Always use *vy* until you are invited to switch, unless addressing a child.

Traditionally, three cheek kisses are given on meeting good friends. This isn't expected from strangers. A firm handshake is more businesslike. Don't offer your hand over the threshold of someone's home or office doorway though, as this is considered bad luck. Some people even prefer not to say "Hello" over the threshold.

INVITATIONS HOME

If you are visiting Belarus for business, it's quite likely that you'll receive an invitation to someone's house on the weekend. Likewise, if you are working with local people via a charity organization or school, they'll enjoy inviting you to join them. The invitation is an honor, and your hosts will take pains to ensure your comfort. Be aware of the effort they have gone to, and show proper appreciation. There's no such thing as popping in for a quick cup of tea, so be ready to dedicate several hours to the experience.

What to Wear

Dressing well is important; Belarusians judge by appearances. A well-cut business suit, shirt, tie, and smart shoes will be right for most occasions. If you want to be more casual, take off your jacket and tie, and undo your top shirt button. Businesswomen can wear a skirt or trouser suit, perhaps with a brightly colored blouse or scarf—Belarusians love color. Local women always wear makeup, so to create a good impression women should use at least a touch of lipstick and a little eye shadow—it's impossible to wear too much.

When being purely casual, anything goes, although Belarusians rarely wear shorts, so having these on will flag you as a tourist. Jeans are the most common attire for both men and women, all year-round, usually teamed with a stylish shirt or glamorous top, rather than a simple T-shirt. If you arrive dressed as you would for a party, you'll probably hit the right note, and your hosts will be pleased that you have made the effort for them.

Bringing a Gift

If you have been invited to somebody's house for a meal, it's a good idea to bring a bottle of wine (Moldovan is particularly popular) or vodka, a cake, a box of chocolates, or a bouquet of flowers—remember, only odd numbers of blooms, as even numbers are just for funerals. If you know that your hosts have children, a small toy also goes over well. Don't be

tempted to kiss a baby on the forehead—this
custom is reserved for corpses. On entering, take
your shoes off; you'll probably be offered a pair of
slippers to wear instead. Not unreasonably, this is
done to help keep the floor clean. If you really
want to impress, take your own slippers.

Food

However humble their circumstances, your hosts
will set out a wonderful buffet in your honor. This
is traditional hospitality—a duty and a pleasure
for the hosts. A typical meal will begin with
zakuski (appetizers) such as salami and pickled
mushrooms. If your hosts are quite well off, there

may be *blini* and *ikra*
(pancakes with caviar).
Remember, this is just the
first course, so don't fill
up. Soup recipes from
Ukraine may follow:
borshch (beetroot based),
solyanka (meaty) or *shchi*
(cabbage). Alternatively, you may be offered
draniki (grated potato pancakes) with
mushrooms and *smetana* (sour cream). *Pirozhki*
(small pasties filled with meat) are also popular,
as are *pelmeni,* the local version of ravioli; these
are often served hot, with butter, but may also be
added to soup.

Needless to say, there will be plenty of bread on
the table: the mainstay of any meal. It's a good
idea to take a little of everything and to praise

every dish. This will please your hostess (who'll have spent several hours in the kitchen). Try not to leave anything on your plate. You will be pressed to take second and third helpings, but just indicate that you are full and no one will be offended. As long as you genuinely give the impression of enjoying the food and appreciating the hospitality, everyone will be happy. Dessert is likely to be a very sweet cake made with artificial cream, or fresh fruit salad. Finally, you'll be offered tea or coffee (the latter is likely to have grounds at the bottom of the cup so don't stir or drain to the end).

The Potato Eaters

Belarusians adore potatoes, particularly in the form of *draniki*. In fact, they eat so many spuds—around 375 pounds (170 kg) per person per year—that their neighbors have nicknamed them "Bulbashi"— potato eaters. Potatoes are such a staple that it's hard to imagine any meal without them. According to the UN Food and Agriculture Association, Belarus grows more potatoes than any other country on earth (Russia is ranked eighteenth).

DRINKING

Soft drinks are always on offer, commonly berry juices and, sometimes, the local specialties of birch juice (made from sap) or *kvass* (a mildly alcoholic fermented bread and fruit drink). Your hosts will probably have sweet red wine and beer on hand but, if you are male, it's most likely that you'll be offered vodka with the meal. "Vodka" is a diminutive of *voda* (water), and means "little water." Originally, it was made by distilling whatever crop was most abundant; now it's made from grain. Sharing a bottle is a sign of friendship and, once it's opened, it is drained dry. As long as you eat plenty of nibbles and keep drinking water alongside your shots, you should be fine. Salty *zakuski*—little snacks such as gherkins, dried fish, and salami are the perfect accompaniment. An unusual treat is *salo*—lumps of smoked pig fat designed to mop up the alcohol. On first sight, these look rather like cheese.

The local version of sparkling wine (known as *Champagnskoe*) is inexpensive—around US $5 a bottle. It is, of course, drunk at New Year and at weddings, but is a common choice for all celebrations. While the men drink vodka, the women tend to prefer bubbly. Those accustomed to the sparkling wines of Italy, France, Australia, or the USA may not find it to their taste.

Toasting

Toasting has set rituals. When being formal, the first toast is made to the guest of honor. The second is for friends and the third is to women, praising their beauty and talents. You can toast any occasion or object (except the deceased at a funeral). Toasting a new car or fur coat is a charming local custom, showing appreciation of good fortune. Glasses are filled while on the table. Raise your glass during a toast, clink glasses with everyone (a show of friendship and trust), keep eye contact, then down your vodka in one gulp. Don't let your glass touch the table again until it's empty. In military circles, it's traditional to toast the award of a medal: you place it in a glass of vodka, drain the spirit, then remove the decoration and put it on.

CONVERSATION

When meeting someone for the first time, safe topics of conversation include the weather and how delighted you are to be in Belarus—how beautiful it is, how clean, safe, and well-organized, how friendly the people are, and so on. No one will think you are being insincere; they will take it for granted that you are impressed by their country and will enjoy hearing your thoughts. Don't stray into criticism; this would not be appreciated, even if those around you secretly agreed. It's one thing for local people, who live with frustrations, to complain about their lives. It's quite another for a foreigner to comment.

Once you know someone a little better, inquiries about health are usual. If your acquaintance mentions that they are feeling unwell you can politely ask if they have seen a doctor or are taking medication. This won't be construed as nosiness but, rather, as appropriate concern. Likewise, if you have a sniffle or remark on feeling tired, expect an analysis of your health!

If you ask what's on at the opera or ballet, or mention a Russian author you've read recently, or a Russian film you've enjoyed, this will distinguish you as a person of substance and culture. Knowledge of any Belarusian poets, authors, or films will elicit a positively glowing response. If you're a sports fan, talking about Belarusian sporting success will go over well. Belarusians are so thoughtful and accommodating that if you express a particular interest you may well find yourself invited to a game, or concert, or show.

The one topic of conversation that is best avoided is politics. Your colleagues won't feel easy about giving their opinions, even once they know you quite well. Don't lead anyone into saying something they may later regret. If your contacts work for a state-run company, they will undoubtedly be full of praise for it—they can hardly say anything else. You may need to read between the lines and rely on your own judgment.

Old Soviet Saying Still Recalled in Belarus
Don't think it.
If you think it, don't say it.
If you say it, don't write it.
If you write it, don't sign it.
If you sign it, don't be surprised.

Belarusian men are "all male," so won't appreciate your admiring or complimenting them on their accessories. They may well go to some lengths to look smart—with an eye-catching tie, fancy watch, and fashionable shoes—but they don't seek compliments, especially from male colleagues. Overt interest will only make them uncomfortable.

Alone, close friends are likely to talk about family matters and problems at work, with women discussing the state of their marriage or their love life. Lighthearted conversation is often anecdotal, recalling humorous stories from their shared past, or might involve an exchange of views on a film, book, or play. The conversation can easily turn philosophical.

Belarusian women commonly see foreign men as good husband material, believing they are rich and can offer them a comfortable life. Online dating agencies have enabled countless numbers of young girls to "meet" husbands from abroad. Many of those taking English classes do so with the express wish of getting hitched to an American or British man. Men, be aware that, regardless of how charming you believe yourself to be, you are the hunted, not the hunter.

chapter five

DAILY LIFE

Belarusians appreciate the simple things in life: a warm home, food on the table, a steady job, friendship, and family. They tend not to have grand aspirations, and ambition has as many negative connotations as positive, implying an inclination to step unfairly over colleagues to climb the ladder. They help neighbors, are kindhearted, and, once they become your friend, will go out of their way to be hospitable. Belarusians adore their children and often overindulge them, particularly since most families have only one child.

However, the old Soviet mentality still reigns supreme in many ways. Belarusians are wary of those they don't know. They'll refrain from familiarity until they trust you, so don't expect strangers to smile at you on the street. If you smile at or greet people you don't know, they'll assume you are soft in the head. Similarly, service in shops and even cafés can be dreadful. In days gone by you were supposed to be grateful for any service at all and were in no position to make demands. Attitudes are slowly changing, but don't be surprised if staff intentionally ignore you or roll their eyes when you persist in asking for help.

A TYPICAL HOME

Around 75 percent of urban housing and many village homes were destroyed during the Second World War. Drab but functional high-rise accommodation was quickly put up to alleviate the problem; much of it still stands, becoming increasingly less attractive as the decades pass. This chronic shortage was recently exacerbated by the need to resettle Chernobyl victims.

In 1993, per capita housing stood at around 205 square feet (around 19 sq. m). Rural homes offer more space but often lack indoor bathrooms or central heating. Increasingly, young people are leaving rural areas to seek a new life in the towns, placing even more pressure on urban housing and public transportation systems.

The center of Minsk was restored in a pleasing fashion, with its classical facades beautifully adorned with ornate balconies and other decorative details. Inside, they are a different matter. Hallways and corridors are consistently unpleasant: paint peeling from the walls, a smell of urine, horrifying spaghetti loops of electrical wiring, no lighting, and windows thick with dust and cobwebs. In both public and private buildings, state cleaners come in to mop the floors with bleach every few weeks, leaving an

asphyxiating fug in their wake. Apartments in the city center are, naturally, extremely sought after. You must either pay a huge sum to acquire one or be fortunate enough to inherit one from a relative. Property prices are rocketing at a truly alarming rate, placing them beyond the reach of most workers. The waiting lists for state accommodation remain long (people may wait up to fifteen years to be housed). Many families purchased their apartments a few years ago, having been given the option to buy their (often crumbling) rented state housing.

Due to this shortage of affordable housing, young people are often obliged to live with their parents until their late twenties and beyond, even after marriage and having children. It's not uncommon to find three generations sharing a three-room apartment, all rooms being used for both sleeping and living. Kitchens and bathrooms tend to be old-fashioned, unchanged since their installation several decades previously. Most Belarusians living in the capital reside in the high-rise blocks of the suburbs. A cluster of buildings will commonly have an open space in the center, with some ancient playground equipment. The public transportation system serving these suburbs is being placed under increasing strain. The government is well aware of the situation, and is making efforts to invest in new apartment building while expanding infrastructure to meet the needs of burgeoning areas.

THE FAMILY
Marriage

Unlike many of their European counterparts, Belarusian women have yet to shake off the shackles of housework. Most hold down a full-time job while also doing the shopping, cooking, cleaning, and laundry for their families. Men certainly don't expect to help out. Although women take a natural pride in their ability to "multitask," there is a strong feeling among younger women that there has to be more to life. They are increasingly realizing that marriage to a Belarusian man isn't all it's cracked up to be, especially as alcoholism and domestic violence rear their ugly heads all too often.

Alcoholism is a real problem for Belarusians, especially in depressed rural areas. Men's average life expectancy of just sixty-four years (compared to seventy-six for women) is an indicator of a cavalier attitude toward their own health. Overindulgence is a major turnoff for most Belarusian women; when asked what they are looking for in a husband, they commonly list sobriety in their top three criteria. However, many men now take more exercise and are switching from liquor to beer. Belarus's beer market is one of the fastest growing in Eastern Europe.

Belarusian men are also known for their philandering ways, marriage being seen as no obstacle to having a bit of fun on the side. The romance of marrying young prevails, however, quite often leading to divorce in the late twenties or early thirties. Reasons cited for divorce tend to focus on husbands' infidelity and reluctance to help around the house. Since men move directly from being looked after by their mothers to being cared for by their wives, it's hardly surprising they don't leap to do the washing up. Second, and even third, marriages are not uncommon, though. Increasingly, young women are tempted into dating foreign men via the Internet, convinced that a better deal must surely be available.

Children

Belarus's demographic crisis is being tackled head-on by an aggressive government campaign to encourage women to start their families early. In 2006 the "Year of the Mother" saw numerous TV programs, books, award ceremonies, concerts, and art exhibitions devoted to the theme. Various financial incentives continue to be offered and motherhood is still frequently lauded as a woman's "sacred duty." Although the president has exhorted women to have three children each to avoid demographic disaster, few yet seem convinced—the benefits currently available are not enough to offset the inconvenience of finding living space for a large family or a woman's inevitable loss of income.

Family Meals

At breakfast time, children usually have porridge (*kasha*) or an omelet. Adults will have the same or, if in a hurry, might take a slice of bread with some cheese and meat. At lunchtime, those who work in large factories or government buildings can use their cafeteria for a half-hour meal— soup, minced meat cutlets, and mayonnaise-covered salads are popular. Some might grab something from the local corner shop in between running a few errands: a pastry, fruit, yogurt, or bread rolls. Those with more freedom to take a leisurely lunch—such as independent businessmen and higher government officials— will happily relax over a two-hour meal.

Families still gather together at the table for their evening meal, although the TV might well be on in the background. Soup is the most common first course in winter, with cooked meat, vegetables, and potatoes (or occasionally rice or pasta) to follow. In summer, salami and salads are popular.

Although local supermarkets are void of many of the processed foods that are causing obesity elsewhere in the world, the Belarusian diet tends to rely heavily on carbohydrates. Eggs and fatty salamis are the most popular sources of protein. State surveys have found that few people buy fish or the better cuts of meat and chicken, as these are relatively expensive.

WORK

Most Belarusians want an easy job; they don't generally seek extra responsibility. Opportunities for promotion are limited, especially for women, and performance-related pay is not yet operational. Office workers tend to start at 9:00 a.m., and leave by 5:30 or 6:00 p.m., while shift work is common in factories and essential services. The EU has been placing pressure on Belarus to give its workers labor rights comparable to those found in the rest of Europe. At present, it is illegal to be a member of an unregistered (that is, non-state controlled) trade union.

EDUCATION

Standards of education are quite high, with almost 99 percent of fifteen-to-twenty-four-year-olds classed as literate. Meanwhile, ever-greater numbers are pursuing further education, which is subsidized well by the state: 74 percent of girls and 54 percent of boys (UNESCO figures for 2005). The curriculum is taught in a very traditional way, however, with the accent placed on remembering facts rather than encouraging lateral thinking.

Preschool

Most parents send their preschool children to kindergarten from the age of four to six, often as a convenient form of day care. In 2005, 91.5 percent of urban preschool children attended and 50.5 percent of rural children. Plans are under way to extend the availability of kindergartens countrywide as they are seen as preparation for primary school. You'll notice long lines of children walking hand-in-hand along the sidewalk toward their nearest park, accompanied by a teacher front and back; fresh air is as important as art and music for these little ones, alongside learning simple school skills.

General Education

Children must attend school between the ages of six and eighteen. Paradoxically, Russian is the most common medium of instruction, with Belarusian usually taught as a separate subject. In 1994, there were 220 schools in Minsk whose language of instruction was Belarusian. Two years later, their number had shrunk to fewer than twenty. The curriculum includes "ideology" lessons, focusing on patriotic duty rather than the Marxist–Leninism of Soviet times.

Special education within the general education system is given to 53.2 percent of children with physical or mental challenges. Those with more severe difficulties attend specialized schools. At the age of sixteen, students have a choice between further academic study and following a vocational course, such as learning to become an electrician, plumber, or builder.

Higher Education

The Belarusian House of Representatives has announced that their long-term goal is for all higher education students to become fee-paying (currently around 60 percent pay fees). Low-interest educational loans will be offered to those who need them. In early 2007, over 6,000 foreign students were studying in Belarus (many from

CIS countries, China, India, and the Middle East). The government hopes to raise this number significantly by 2010, enabling the system to subsidize local students. Belarusian

students pay around $1,000 for their tuition, while foreign citizens pay up to $3,500.

On graduating, those who have had their fees paid by the state are obliged to teach in rural schools for two years. This goes some way toward solving the shortage of teachers in unpopular areas.

The Belarusian Language Society is keen to establish a Belarusian National University (BNU), securing students the right to be educated in Belarusian. However, this choice is commonly viewed as "pro-opposition" (see Chapter 9, Communicating: Russian versus Belarusian).

The Belarusian Republican Youth Union

In Soviet days, children became "Pioneers" at nine and "Komsomol" members at sixteen. Around 60 percent of the present adult population would have been members. Belarus's own modern version (the Belarusian Republican Youth Union) aims to promote patriotism and instill moral values via activities such as camping, sports, and visiting memorials, and is the largest youth group in Belarus. The president criticizes university staff who complain of state campaigns to persuade young people to join, saying they should quit if they don't agree. "Young people should support the country's leadership," says Mr. Lukashenko.

MILITARY SERVICE

Overall, there are about 65,000 personnel in the armed forces, with conscripts outweighing professionals. At the age of eighteen, young men are obliged to fulfill their national service duties for eighteen months, with the option of extension. Those going to university can defer their service but it must be completed by the age of twenty-seven. Naturally, most are reluctant to leave the comforts of home, where they are spoiled by doting mothers. Additionally, stories abound of young soldiers being bullied by older recruits—a practice common from Soviet times. In recent years, growing numbers have been exempt from service as medically unfit. A drive to encourage women to volunteer has also been undertaken, with some success.

WEEKENDS

At the end of the working week, most women catch up on the laundry, cleaning, and shopping. Men gravitate toward the television. The classic Belarusian scenario is that men spend the weekend watching sport and drinking beer. Those

 of a slightly more active disposition will go to an ice hockey match or meet up with pals at the *banya* (see Chapter 6, Time Out). Teenagers, courting couples, and

newlyweds are a different matter: they are the ones promenading, going to the theater, and sitting in cafés. Children are often taken to the park or, as a special treat, to the circus. In the winter months, hardy men go ice fishing and athletic types strap on their skis.

Summer offers other diversions. Whole families will cram themselves into the car to go to their *dacha*. This is when mushroom-picking mania sets in. Together, they'll happily spend a few hours hunting for fungi, or wild berries, which they preserve to sustain them through the long winter. A walk in the forest fills the Belarusian soul with delight. Most Belarusians are great nature-lovers and pride themselves on being able to identify birdsong and wild flowers.

The Joys of Mushroom Hunting

"There's a special pleasure in wandering through white-barked birch groves. Rays of sunshine dapple the soft moss underfoot and not a single discontented thought enters your head. What is more thrilling than the joy of discovering a patch of young brown boletus? Of course, it's not just mushrooms you'll find in the woods, but mental repose. You return home refreshed, your soul cleansed from all worry and care."
(As related by a Belarusian friend.)

Barbecued *shashlyk* kebabs (a Georgian dish) are a must, with Belarusians hardly able to speak of this delicacy without licking their lips. Indeed, when they are prepared well, they are delicious. Every Belarusian cook has his or her own favorite marinade recipe.

Most weekends are spent in these ways, and some even retreat to their *dachas* for several weeks at a time over these warmer months. Holidays at state-run spas, often set picturesquely beside lakes, are also much looked forward to.

EVERYDAY SHOPPING

Most people shop several times a week, picking up their daily items from their local corner shop (*producti*). A few hypermarkets have just opened in the major cities and those with cars are beginning to venture to them for a larger shop, but most people aren't yet ready to abandon the mindset of simply purchasing what they need as they need it. This probably makes sense if you are trying to live within a tight budget. There's no question that most food

items are expensive, especially when local salaries are considered. Shopping in Vilnius, the capital of Lithuania, is almost 50 percent cheaper. Although the shelves of Belarusian shops are never empty, as a foreigner you may

find it difficult to find much that you want to buy. Goods tend to be drab: gray toilet paper, cheap pasta and rice, rather tasteless salami, endless jars of pickled vegetables, gherkins, bags of smoked fish, and bland cheese. Making a meal from what's on offer can seem quite a challenge. There are very few goods imported from outside the CIS, although you can usually find a good selection of tea and coffee.

Belarusian favorites, such as *salo*, pickled fish, and preserved mushrooms, cabbage, beetroot, and gherkins are unlikely to tempt the Western palate, and cheese, fish, and meat often look unappetizing.

You may prefer to eat out, as the better restaurants always seem to offer tastier food than the shops.

Shopping Tips

- Bring your own bags with you, or you will be charged up to US $0.20 for a flimsy plastic one that will split if you put more than a few items into it.
- If you walk in with bags from other shops, you must check them into a locker. Keep your handbag with you, and ensure nothing valuable is left in your checked bags. You'll often receive a shopping basket in return, which you must take with you after you finish at the register, as you'll need it to retrieve your original bags.
- If you are buying fresh fruit and vegetables, you may need to hand your items to an assistant to be weighed. If the shop is busy, it's every man for himself; don't be too polite, or you'll be there all day. The same goes for catching the attention of anyone behind the fish, meat, or deli counters.
- Don't place money directly into someone's hand, since this is viewed as unlucky (the receiver "takes" the other's ability to earn money). There are small dishes next to the cashier for you to deposit your notes into (there are no coins in Belarus). If you try to give money directly, you'll often be ignored. Change is also placed in the dish, regardless of whether you've put out your hand to receive it. Try to keep small notes handy, as cashiers often run low on these.

- Shops are usually open from around 8:00 a.m. until 8:00 p.m. or later. On Sundays, shorter hours are usual. There are a few hypermarkets, such as Gippo, springing up, but smaller supermarkets and corner shops remain the norm. Government controls mean that prices are similar everywhere, and there is rarely an advantage in buying larger quantities; this ensures a fair deal for those unable to travel far or who can't afford to buy in bulk.

- You'll find some unfamiliar dairy items ready to trip you up as you hunt for a simple carton of milk (*moloko*) or cream (*slivki*). Belarusians love drinkable yogurt (*kefir*), sour cream (*smetana*), and a host of other condensed and processed milk products. You may find that you love them too, but this won't be much comfort if you've just poured them unwittingly into your breakfast tea. The solution is to try them out. You may be familiar with cottage cheese (*tvorok*), but may not have tried it wrapped in chocolate, with jam in the middle!

- Black bread is a specialty; locals adore it, but you may find it rather hard and chewy. Cheap white sliced bread is also freely available, but it's tasteless, and usually quite stale. A few upscale venues sell delicious soft loaves; these are more expensive than "local" bread. Since preservatives aren't used, however, they will stay fresh for two days at the most. The same goes for anything you buy in a jar—once it's opened, it has a very short shelf life.

At the Market

Each suburb of Minsk has its own small outdoor *rinok* (market), selling colorful fruit and vegetables, eggs, jars of preserves and pickles, and dried goods. You won't find meat, fish, or a wide selection of perishable dairy goods, though. Komorovsky Rinok (Y. Kolas metro) in the center of town is the place to go, with its indoor and outdoor stalls open every day except Monday. Produce here tends to be fresher than in the supermarkets, simply because of the greater turnover. Fruit and vegetables past their best are marked down. Watch out for traders slipping bruised items in with your good ones, though. Prices are set but, if you buy several kilos, sellers may generously throw in a few extra items. The beautiful displays of berries outside are a real treat in summer; the smell is heavenly. Inside, the meat counters aren't always as delightful, although you may marvel at the pigs' heads and trotters. Try  to hand over the right money; you won't want to put change in your purse, as it will be sticky with blood.

Provincial cities also have their own markets, often partially housed indoors. Even the smallest towns have outdoor produce stalls, where small-scale growers can bring their modest crops for sale, vying for trade with more established sellers.

chapter six

TIME OUT

Belarusians love to get together with friends. For the younger generation, this often translates to a stroll through town and a leisurely stop at a small café. Men of all ages are football and ice hockey fans, ensuring matches are well attended, and lots of young Belarusians play for local teams. The only sport that really endures through middle age is skiing—usually cross-country. The state heavily subsidizes and promotes cultural events such as art exhibitions, opera, ballet, concerts, and the circus, and most Minskites attend several times a year. Eating out at a restaurant is quite a treat, with canteen-style cafés offering a reasonable alternative. Belarus doesn't have a bar culture. Instead, people usually invite friends to their homes. A big night out, even for the middle-aged, involves a trip to a nightclub. And there is always the *banya* (sauna)—a traditional place to catch up on gossip while purifying body, mind, and soul.

PROMENADING

Central Minsk has a style all of its own, a product of Soviet planning at its most inspired, with immense avenues, impressive panoramas, and reconstructed colonnaded neoclassical facades making it a wonderful place for promenading. Teenagers sometimes meet in mixed groups but most choose same-sex friends, enjoying seeing and being seen. By night, Minsk is beautifully illuminated—perfect for young lovers taking a romantic meander. On weekends, young families set off for the parks. The older generation tend not to walk purely for pleasure; they are usually only on their way to and from work or the *producti* shop.

If you happen upon an opposition demonstration during your stroll, it's wise not to linger or look too interested. Your nationality won't deter the police from arresting you.

CHURCHES AND RELIGIOUS ART

Belarus boasts numerous ancient churches, many of which are being restored and brought back into use. They are well worth visiting. The country also has a history of producing beautiful icons; the art is still taught at St. Yelisavetinsky Monastery. Several icons housed in Belarusian places of worship are said to have miraculous powers, such as weeping myrrh before times of calamity.

The Red Church, otherwise known as the St. Simon and Elena Cathedral, is a famous

Minsk landmark near the Hotel Minsk. It opened in 1910 but housed the BSSR State Polish Theater after the October Revolution. In the postwar years, it became home to the Sovietskaya Belarus Film Studio and only reopened to worshipers after Independence.

Other sites worth visiting include Nesvizh's Corpus Christi Church, with its baroque frescoes and a spooky crypt with the remains of nobles past; Polotsk's eleventh-century Sofia Cathedral and St. Efrasinnia's Monastery, founded in 1125; Grodno's Pokrovsky and Farny Cathedrals on Sovietskaya Square; and Zhirovitsa's glorious fifteenth-century Monastery of the Assumption, whose cathedral houses a Holy Mother icon renowned for its miraculous powers.

PARKS

Gorky Park is for children. During the summer, costumed dancers, singers, and amateur groups perform. A small train wends its way through the park, and there are fairground rides, including a

Ferris wheel, for all ages. The Botanic Gardens offer a wilder experience. This is a pleasant place for a stroll, and you can forget you're in the center of the city. There are wooded pathways, formal planting, and greenhouses. Next door is the vast forested area of Chelyuskintsev Park. Many smaller parks are found throughout the city, with imposing sculptures—solid relics of Belarus's Soviet past—or modern, whimsical pieces.

EATING OUT
Belarusian Cuisine
Belarusians love their soups. If you have a sweet tooth, you'll like *borshch* (beetroot based), and *solyanka* appeals to meat lovers. A staple is *draniki* (fried grated potato pancakes), which tend to be rather greasy but taste amazingly good. They can be served with almost anything, but a creamy mushroom sauce is most usual. Try some *pirozhki* meat pies, or *pelmeni,* which is like ravioli.

Have a glass of birch juice (the refreshing sap is extracted from stems in March and April by cutting the bark) or *kvass* (mildly alcoholic, made from brown bread soaked in water, sugar, mint, and fruit). They can be homemade, but there are several commercially available brands. Belarus is famous for its local vodka, which many consider to be superior to Russian brands. Minsk's Krystal is one of the most highly respected and is among the oldest of the former USSR, established in 1893. Belarus is, amazingly, the fifth-largest consumer of vodka in the world, with annual consumption of over 14.5 million cases. When ordering vodka, don't forget the appetizers (*zakuski*), or you may end up rather inebriated. These range from simple plates of salami and gherkins to elaborately displayed mayonnaise-covered salads. *Blini* and *ikra* (pancakes with caviar) are just as popular here as they are in Russia. *Salo* (smoked pork fat) is particularly effective, and in some places is served wrapped around assorted vegetable fillings.

Belarusian Balsam also deserves a mention. This thick, dark syrup is recommended for sore throats and flu; it tastes unpleasantly medicinal to the Western palate but, in tea with honey, it has its own charm. Belovezhskaya Bitters are similarly herbal and have a high alcohol content.

In recent years, the police have taken an active role in uncovering the brewing of illegal moonshine (known as *samogon*). The only places to have a license for production are the national park of the Belovezhaya Puscha and the folk museum village of Dudutki. Hundreds of home distilleries have been closed, but the situation remains acute. The spirit is so potent that even moderate consumption can lead to alcohol poisoning. Beware when outside the big cities.

Vodka—the Cure for All Ills

To cure a fever, rub vodka on your chest and feet or, before bed, stand naked—except for a woolen hat—with your feet in a bowl of hot water, and drink a large mug of honeyed tea containing at least two measures of vodka. Soaking your feet in vodka is supposed to cure smelliness, and washing your hair with it is said to ward off dandruff. You can gargle with it for a sore throat, place it in your ear to cure earache, and even use it to clean mold off the wall!

Restaurants and Cafés

Belarusians don't have a bar culture as such, since they usually drink while eating. There are a couple of restaurants in the center of Minsk that have a barlike atmosphere, but few customers go there merely to drink. However, it's quite common to see people walking along the street with a bottle of beer, even at the start of the day. Beer is seen as a soft drink, in contrast to vodka, is cheap, and widely sold. In summer, every bench is filled with youngsters chatting and swigging the local beer.

Don't rely on there being English menus. If you strike it rich, you can amuse yourself reading the consistently atrocious translations. Prices vary greatly around town. You can go to a cafeteria-style establishment and have three courses for US $5 or to a plush restaurant and have a super meal for US $30. Imported beers and wines are pricey, particularly Italian and French wines. It is no cheaper to buy a bottle than simply to pay by the glass, so the latter is advisable. Minsk still has only a small number of good restaurants, so they get busy. Do book your table in advance. The Singing Fountain, located some way behind the football stadium, is among the best. If you're out for the evening, you may find your chosen eatery has live music or even a show; exotic or cabaret dancing is quite common. If you feel this might make your own party uncomfortable, you can check in advance, but your Belarusian contacts won't bat an eyelid—they love it. There are quite a few cafés in the center of town. Several are found along Nezavisimosti Avenue (Independence Avenue), on the opposite side from the Hotel Minsk. London Café is a particular delight, with miniature models of London sights inside. The News Café and My English Granny's Café—both opposite the British Embassy on Karl Marx Street—are a great choice, whether for a quick coffee or a full meal. Minsk has two breweries: Krynitsa and Alevaria. Both have been doing well in the local market, producing light and dark beers of various strengths, and are seeing exports grow. Russian Baltica is more expensive, but remains the beer of choice for many wealthier beer lovers. Minsk also has two microbreweries, producing their own delicious brews and selling them via their rustic-styled restaurants. Rakovski Brovar is at 10 Vitebskaya Street, and Staroe Ruslo is at 7 Ulyanauskaya, near the stadium.

Standards of service aren't always what you'd wish. You may find yourself waiting some time to order and again for your drinks to arrive. Try to avoid becoming stressed by the nonchalance around you. Note that asking for individual bills is unheard of. In restaurants, be prepared to treat your fellow diners, split the cost evenly, or work it out laboriously yourself.

TIPPING

Service charges are not automatically added, but tipping is entirely discretionary. In restaurants and cafés, a 5 percent tip is adequate. Taxi drivers and hotel staff don't generally expect tips, so if you want to give something it will be appreciated.

MUSEUMS AND GALLERIES

Don't miss the chance to see Minsk's Great Patriotic War Museum on October Square; the Belarusians claim it to be the first museum dedicated exclusively to the Second World War. Although the information isn't displayed in English, it's easy to understand most of what you are looking at. Photos of public hangings and Jewish extermination horrors are particularly disturbing. German maps reveal the Nazis' plans for mass killing, with projected figures showing that 75 percent of Belarusians were to be annihilated. Local travel agencies will also be happy to provide you with a guide if you wish to explore Minsk's old ghetto, where over 100,000 Belarusian Jews were gathered during the occupation.

The newly extended National Museum of Art on Lenin Street has a collection of Belarusian art:

modern works; landscapes and portraits from the seventeenth to the twentieth century, including paintings of Belarus's famous Radziwill family; and a beautiful collection of iconography dating back to the fifteenth century. It also has Russian and Western European art, Persian rugs, and Japanese pieces. The small gallery under the Palace of the Republic changes its exhibitions regularly; these can include anything from modern photography to tapestry and ceramics.

Just outside Minsk, you'll find Dudutki, an outdoor folk museum celebrating Belarusian country life, and the Strochitsy Museum, home to over a hundred relocated old buildings.

WAR MEMORIALS

It suits the current regime to keep the horrors of war in the minds of the populace. Although it's widely recognized that international liaisons are vital to ensure trade, people are generally encouraged to be a little wary of foreigners. By remaining insular, the president can continue to exert astonishing influence over the country. Accordingly, every opportunity is taken to glorify the heroic efforts of Belarus's partisans and soldiers during the war years and to remind everyone that unity is the best way to overcome adversity. There are several memorial sites around the capital and nearby.

In addition to the monument in Victory Square and the Afghan memorial on the Isle of Tears, the Khatyn memorial complex is a must. In 1943, in revenge for a nearby partisan attack on Nazi soldiers, Khatyn's villagers were locked in a barn and burned alive. Its twenty-six chimneys have been turned into belfries, each marking the location of a house; they toll the hours, and a plaque on each one commemorates the family members who died. Three birch trees stand by an eternal flame that symbolizes the one in four Belarusians who lost their lives in the war. Six hundred and seventeen other settlements shared the same fate; a handful of soil has been brought from each, and a symbolic "graveyard" lists the villages. It's a chilling place.

The historic town of Novogrudok has two museums: the House Museum of Adam

Mickiewicz, the great Polish-Lithuanian Romantic poet, and the Regional Museum, showing the multinational and multireligious history of the area. The latter includes the Museum of Jewish Resistance, situated on the site of the former ghetto. The exhibition is devoted to the two unprecedented acts of resistance by the Jews of Novogrudok during the Nazi occupation—the successful escape of 250 ghetto prisoners through a tunnel they had built themselves, and the largest Jewish partisan detachment in Europe headed by Tuvia Bielski. There is a partisan camp in the forest outside the village of Chereshlya, and a Partisan Museum in the village itself.

The Mount of Glory, an impressive memorial on the outskirts of Minsk, is also worth a visit. Three huge bayonets, rimmed by a mosaic depicting the horrors of war, stand high on a hill made from soil brought from all over Belarus.

OPERA, BALLET, CIRCUS, AND THEATER

Belarus has a rich and varied cultural life. There is a tradition of encouraging young talent—in academic achievement, art, music, dance, and sport. Some attend prestigious specialized

schools; others go to after-school clubs or take private lessons. A surprising number of people play a musical instrument, and you'll often find that acquaintances were once on a junior team of some kind. This promotes a common love of the arts. Few Belarusians miss the opportunity to attend a concert or go to the ballet.

Minsk's Opera House, currently being renovated, is located next to the grand facade of the Ministry of Defense. The 1930s building may look rather ugly from the outside but its painted and gilt interior is awe-inspiring. Operatic sets tend to be kept simple, but the singing won't disappoint. The orchestra is also excellent. Minsk's ballet troupe is not the equal of Moscow's Bolshoi ballet company but, in contrast to the opera, its costumes and sets are lavish. Both are subsidized, enabling people to attend for a mere $4 or less. Some ballet performances outshine others; if you catch them on a bad day, you may find the chorus out of sync and the lead dancers wobbling. Nevertheless, it's certainly something to be experienced, even if you aren't usually a fan. The opera and ballet have a rolling program so, if you miss *Carmen*, *The Nutcracker*, or *Swan Lake*, don't despair—they'll soon be back.

Belarus's Philharmonic Orchestra is much praised and there are several other musical groups that put on regular performances. Folk dancing and traditional music are a huge draw. During the summer, an outside stage is often set up on October Square for state holidays; top orchestral groups, folk-dancing ensembles, and the operatic company perform throughout the day. The parks commonly host amateur dance and music groups through the warmer months.

There are several theaters in Minsk, including one opposite the President's Palace, near October Square. They show classic Molière, Shakespeare, and Chekhov, and also modern plays by Russian and Belarusian writers—never in English, though. Minsk doesn't generally attract big international rock and pop stars, because the ticket revenue isn't adequate. However, it has welcomed ELO and The Cardigans in recent years.

You can buy tickets from the "box office" located in the Nezavisimosti underpass next to McDonald's. The agency sells tickets to every concert and show in Minsk, all reasonably priced.

The circus is highly popular and respected, with several shows each week. Although half the audience is under the age of eight, this is also regarded as suitable adult entertainment. If you don't like to see performing animals, don't go, but then you will miss the excellent acrobats. Opened in 1959, it was the largest circus in the USSR. It seats 1,668, and still boasts the bronze chandeliers presented by Moscow's Light Bulb Works.

NIGHTCLUBS

There is a fairly big nightclub scene in Minsk, with most venues doubling as restaurants early in the evening. It's advisable to prebook a table if you want to go on a Saturday night, although this commonly involves a minimum spend of around US $30 per head. Toward midnight a floor show is usual, with anything from gypsy performers to feathered cabaret girls or chunky male strippers. Then the disco lasts all night. Some clubs offer billiards; others have casinos. Expect traditional Russian pop rather than American or British hits. The clubs certainly offer a glamorous break from the norm.

If you like dancing, try out a variety of clubs: you're sure to find something that suits you. Zhuravinka is a stylish, expensive club that caters perfectly to work parties or other groups, and couples in their forties. Goodwin's is popular with students, while Bronx attracts the beautiful people. Hotel Belarus's Westworld Club (aka Shaiba) is large and busy and tends to attract businessmen with young female companions. For imaginative décor and a more European vibe, head to X-ray at 27 Internationalnaya. Expect to pay at least US $10 for entry, and more to secure a table. Be ready for heaving dance floors— Belarusians enjoy themselves with abandon.

THE *BANYA*

The Belarusians love their *banyas* (steam baths). Most people go at least once a month, some every week. Those with *dachas* often have a *banya* in the garden. In days gone by, the *banya* was primarily a communal washing place: many people, even in

Minsk, didn't have their own bathrooms until a few decades ago. In town, there is a huge choice. You can go to a public *banya* (around US $1 to US $2) to share the experience with around thirty others, or pay a lot more to attend a private *banya*. Small rooms can usually be rented, catering to four to eight people at a time. This is more private, of course, and encourages people to use the rooms for discussing business, or just to share some gossip. Men and women usually attend separately, partly because it's traditional to go nude, but also because they like to use the time to meet up with old friends.

There are many rituals associated with the *banya*. It is common to wear a rimmed felt hat to protect your head from the heat. Once you've steamed yourself, you're supposed to douse yourself in icy water—or jump in a lake if you're in the countryside. The shocking change in temperature stimulates your circulatory system and, it's thought, your immune system. You also beat each other with damp twigs to encourage the circulation. It may sound like a hellish ordeal, but it's actually very relaxing. Women often combine the *banya* with beauty routines: face masks, hair dyeing, leg shaving, and so on. For the authentic deal, Minsk's *Banya* Number One is perfect. You'll find a wonderful cross-section of the public here, from children accompanying their parents to lithe young things and ancient grannies. After a few hours of sweating and scrubbing, you'll float out feeling pounds lighter.

SPORTS

In their desire for the body beautiful, most young Belarusians do some form of exercise. For men, this might be a twice-weekly trip to lift weights at the gym. Women tend to combine aerobics classes with gym sessions, or go to yoga classes. There are plenty of private fitness clubs, with membership from around $50 per month; these tend to offer dance and exercise classes too. Swimming is also a popular choice. There are several public baths and a few very smart private ones. For most, you have to present a local doctor's certificate stating that you are in good health.

Tennis is the latest craze for young Belarusians, perhaps inspired by the international success of Minsk's own Max Mirnyi (ranked number one men's doubles player in 2007). There is a huge tennis complex near the center of Minsk, and there are some outdoor courts behind the Circus.

In winter, outdoor ice rinks are popular. The one in October Square gets very busy. You can rent skates for next to nothing. There is an indoor rink in Gorky Park all year-round.

Cross-country skiing is one of the biggest winter pastimes, and downhill skiing is also gaining popularity, largely due to two new skiing centers just outside Minsk: Silichi and Logoisk. These offer accommodation, saunas, cafés, ice rinks, and man-made slopes—with artificial snow if the weather won't oblige. They are pleasant places to pass a day or a weekend. You can rent skis, boots, and poles cheaply, but need your own outfit. You can also go to Raubichi (half an hour's drive from the center of the capital) to watch Belarus's ski jumpers in training. The other winter pastime is ice fishing. It's hard to imagine why sitting in the middle of a freezing lake or river seems attractive, and accidents do happen when people misjudge the thickness of the ice, but this is an enduringly popular sport among men.

Belarus's most famous sporting figure is Grodno gymnast Olga Korbut, who won four gold medals and two silver at the Summer Olympics of 1972 and 1976 as part of the Soviet team. Other sporting heroes include the sprinter Yulia Nesterenko from Brest, who took the Olympic gold at Athens in 2004. At the Sydney 2000 Olympics, Yekaterina Karsten took gold for rowing, Yanina Korolchik for shot put, and Ellina Zvereva for discus.

The national teams do well in weightlifting, wrestling, women's gymnastics, equestrian events, and the biathlon. Achieving success at the prestigious international events—such as the Olympic Games—is hugely significant to the state. A great deal of money is invested in keeping facilities up-to-date and in encouraging youngsters to fulfill their sporting potential. All Belarus's major towns have sports complexes.

Ice hockey is the most popular team game, drawing great crowds, and several of Belarus's top players are on loan to the Canadian League. When

big tournaments are on, it can be difficult to secure tickets. Catch a game at Minsk's Palace of Sports. Football has a much smaller following, but many do follow the success of Belarusian teams. Minsk's Dynamo team regularly plays at its stadium in the center of town and sometimes hosts international games. Belarus's Alexander Hleb—known for playing with with London's Arsenal—is a darling of the local media.

SHOPPING FOR PLEASURE

A trip to Minsk's Komarovsky Rinok (Y. Kolas metro) offers a slice of Belarusian life. The

displays of fruit and vegetables are temptingly colorful and aromatic; the aisles of fresh berries in summer are breathtaking.

Minsk's top bakery is Karavai, on Victory Square. It's worth paying a visit just to see their spectacular cakes, laden with decorative frosted flowers in pastel shades. Few emerge without a boxed confection under their arm. Belarusians are particularly fond of chocolate, and have two thriving domestic companies: Spartak and Kommunarka. Their range is impressively large. Dark varieties with nuts, raisins, and liqueurs are especially good. The capital's best-known sweet shop, Lakomka ("Sweet Tooth") is at 19 Independence Avenue. Open the door, and the smell of chocolate will almost overpower you.

For a taste of "Soviet" shopping, pop into Tsum or Gum, both on Independence Avenue. These "department stores" are, in fact, a hodgepodge of market stalls, selling all things imaginable. You can buy locally made electrical goods, toiletries, and clothes, or select a Russian import. Occasionally, items from Poland or China appear. Often, goods are displayed in glass cases or on shelves, so you have to catch the attention of the frosty looking shop assistants in order to inspect something more closely. Although times are changing, the old system of payment is still prevalent, whereby you pay a cashier for your item, collect a receipt, and present this at the counter to collect your purchase. This can be time-consuming, since you may have to stand in line to choose your item, again to pay, and again to collect. Perhaps because of these frustrations, shopping isn't most people's idea of a leisure activity. The underpass near October Square also houses quite a few stalls, most displaying women's clothes—a riot of brightly colored polyester, cheap lace, and fashions you thought were long dead. Music shops (largely selling pirated copies of CDs and DVDs) and florists also abound in these subterranean walkways.

If you need a good winter coat, Zhdanovichi Market, twenty minutes' drive from the center of the capital, is the place to go. You can buy imported fur and leather or locally made woolen coats for bargain prices.

Belarus doesn't have much to offer in the way of souvenirs. Woven straw dolls and linen tablecloths are traditional. You could buy a piece of local artwork from one of the artists' galleries, of which there are several; a large gallery is located almost opposite the Hotel Minsk, and there is an open-air art market next to the War Museum on October Square. This site also hosts a craft market, selling straw and *matrioshka* (stacking) dolls and attractive lacquered boxes depicting fairy-tale scenes. Be ready to haggle. Bulk buying ensures a better deal.

Icy Pleasures

The Belarusians' love of ice cream seems remarkable considering their long, cold winters; they are ever ready to consume it, even when temperatures plummet to well below zero. The habit was remarked upon by the British prime minister Winston Churchill: "People who eat ice cream in winter will never be defeated." During the Cold War, it was commonly joked that the USSR could be proud of three things: missiles, ballet, and—ice cream.

WHAT TO SEE IN MINSK

Although the modern apartment buildings in the suburbs are undeniably ugly, some of the city's new architecture deserves praise. The Palace of the Republic concert hall on October Square, built in 2001, is so dazzlingly stark and monolithic that it commands unfaltering attention.

The new library, opened in 2006, is a huge

polyhedron, jokingly likened to the Death Star of Hollywood fame. After dark, illuminations play over its gleaming surface. The city is amazingly clean, courtesy of an army of vigilant state employed cleaners, and probably among the safest in the world. At all times of year, promenading is a popular pastime. October Square is undeniably grand, containing the looming Palace of the Republic and the classically impressive Trade Unions' Culture Palace. In summer, you can catch

open-air concerts here; in winter, it becomes an outdoor ice rink.

You can take a turn down Karl Marx, Lenin, and Engels Streets, and admire the KGB

building on Nezavisimosti. As you might expect, you shouldn't take photos of any government buildings. Walk to the Troitsky Suburb, along the River Svislach. This is where the "old town" is located, rebuilt in colorful nineteenth-century style. Several attractive churches are to be found in this area and, during the warmer months, you can enjoy a beer at one of the outdoor cafés.

You'll find a monument on the Isle of Tears to those who died during the Soviet invasion of Afghanistan: a Belarusian parachute regiment was the first unit sent into the country. It's a somber reminder of young lives lost, and receives many visitors. In Soviet tradition, newlyweds lay flowers and have their photos taken here as part of their tour of the memorials. You'll also see them at elegant Ploshad Pobedy (Victory Square). This site has a commanding dignity; its tall obelisk is adorned with Minsk's "Hero City" emblem, awarded by the USSR in 1974 for efforts during the Great Patriotic War, and an eternal flame is kept burning. Within two minutes' walk, at 2 Kisleva Street, is the building where Lee Harvey Oswald once lived.

chapter **seven**

TRAVEL, HEALTH, & SAFETY

If you can look on your travel experiences as part of life's broad tapestry, you'll be enriched by your time in Belarus. Buses, streetcars, and the metro offer endless opportunities for people watching; meanwhile, there's nothing like rubbing shoulders and breathing in the atmosphere to give you a sense of belonging. Moreover, public transportation is cheap and runs regularly in the capital. On longer journeys, striking up conversations with strangers is quite acceptable; come well prepared with snacks both for yourself and to share with those around you. Belarus is well served by its moderately priced, though occasionally creaky intercity train and bus network—great, as long as you aren't in a hurry. Seats fill up, so book in advance. Whether traveling by road or rail, you'll soon realize that the countryside lacks much variety. It's very flat, with swamps and fields interspersed by forest.

ARRIVAL

Flying into Belarus is notoriously expensive. You can fly most cheaply direct from London with the national airline, Belavia. Lufthansa comes via

Frankfurt, Austrian Air flies via Vienna, Estonian Air via Tallinn, and Czech Air via Prague. Minsk International airport is a rather soulless place—don't be surprised if you arrive in winter and the heating / lighting isn't on. If you depart from here, be aware that its café facilities are very limited, although it has several duty-free shops.

The airport is 26 miles (42 km) from Minsk, so ask your hotel or travel agent to send a car to meet you if you can. Alternatively, there is a shuttle bus to the Central Bus Terminal in town, which departs hourly (7:00 a.m. to 10:00 p.m.) at a cost of about US $1.40. If you want to be independent, a car rental office operates from the arrivals terminal. If you have ordered a taxi in advance, or can find one when you arrive, it should cost no more than US $30.

Driving over the border can be complicated. Long lines are not unknown, and cars must have the necessary documents. Flying into Lithuania's Vilnius from London is quite cheap, and you can take a train from there. Overnight trains from Warsaw, Moscow, or Kiev are a good option. The recently completed new railway station is conveniently situated in the very center of Minsk. Exits to platforms are on the ground floor. Twenty-four-hour booking offices and currency exchange are on the first floor, and the upper floor has a waiting room, a post-office with international telephone, a pharmacy, and bars. Taxis are always waiting just outside.

Bureaucracy

However you enter Belarus, be ready for your passport to be closely scrutinized. A visa is required, and staying past its expiration date is strictly forbidden. Make sure you allow plenty of time to acquire this prior to your trip. Once in Belarus, you are obliged to register at the local office of the Department of Visas and Registration (OVIR) within three days of arrival; if you are staying in a hotel, they'll take care of this for you, asking for your passport on check-in. If you are staying elsewhere, you must register yourself, or risk a fine on departure.

You'll also need to fill out an immigration card at your point of entry and take out the obligatory medical insurance (charged at a daily rate of around $1 per day). Take note, you are only permitted to bring in one liter of spirits. Unless you are from a former Soviet state, a visa is necessary even for crossing Belarus, for example by train. You can be forcibly removed from a train at the border if you fail to show a valid visa. Transit visas are valid for seventy-two hours, while single-entry "ordinary" visas are valid for thirty days within the period stipulated on the visa. The best option for business travelers is the multiple-entry visa, valid for up to a year with a maximum stay of thirty days each time.

Tourist Information

Belarus has no tourist information centers as we know them. Tourist agencies are liable to be the most helpful, or you can ask at the reception desk of your hotel. There are several Web sites that carry useful information in English (see page 165).

GETTING AROUND
Within the Capital

You can walk around the center of Minsk quite easily; the sidewalks are wide and there are plenty of underpasses. Don't jaywalk; cross roads only at designated crossings. Public transportation is very cheap (about US $0.25 for your journey, regardless of length). There are only two metro lines—simple to use, but they don't cover the whole city. Trains can be crowded but stations are pleasant, decorated with Soviet iconography and marble. Pink plastic metro tokens can be bought inside.

Streetcars and buses are everywhere, but you need to know where you are going. Buy your tickets from street kiosks or on board and punch on entry. Private  minibuses also run along set routes; they'll drop you wherever is convenient and charge around US $0.60, payable on entry. Taxis aren't up to Western standards: the cars are ancient, the seatbelts often don't work, and the drivers race dangerously between lanes, narrowly missing the rear ends of those in front as they repeatedly slam on the brakes. Avoid them totally if you suffer from travel sickness. Make sure the meter is turned on when you start. Licensed cabs have a number painted on the side. They can be ordered by phone and you'll be given their ID so you know your own driver. Hailing vehicles isn't an option, although hitchhikers are sometimes seen outside the cities. Tipping isn't usual, but rounding up for good service will be appreciated.

The Nemiga Metro Station Tragedy

On May 30, 1999, fifty-three young people lost their lives during a crush to enter the metro. People trying to leave the station via the staircase were trampled underfoot by a large crowd coming from above, who had been attending a nearby concert and were hurrying to shelter from a sudden heavy rainstorm. Many more people were hospitalized with serious injuries. Almost all of those who died were school and university students. The memorial to them reads: "Fifty-three scars on the heart of Belarus."

Driving Outside the Capital

Traveling around Belarus isn't easy unless you have a car. Your hotel or travel agent can arrange a car and driver for you at around US $0.35 per km. This is much easier than driving yourself, since local drivers switch lanes erratically and often brake sharply, and licenses are often "bought" rather than earned. The main roads are in good condition, but away from these, potholes are common. The police wave drivers over to check documents; this is routine and shouldn't be a problem. Driving under the influence of alcohol is a serious offense, as is speeding. Winter road conditions are always more hazardous because of the volume of slush. At night, outside urban areas, lighting can be sparse: the exception to this is the road to Minsk from the airport, which is, itself, lit up like a runway.

Long-Distance Buses and Trains
Although most Minskers own cars, long journeys are still sometimes undertaken by public transportation and less wealthy rural families often rely utterly on the rail and bus network for travel. It's advisable to book seats ahead of time from the Eastern Bus Station for intercity and international travel. The Central Bus Station also runs buses to neighboring countries as well as within Minsk. Their fleets have been much updated in recent years, making bus travel a little more comfortable. Buses are cheap but depart infrequently and take forever to reach their destination.

Trains are more expensive but definitely preferable, since they give you the chance to stretch your legs a little. The toilet facilities are rather unsavory but, in general, trains are kept pretty clean and in good working order. A few snacks are always available but it's advisable to bring your own, plus drinks. Trains, which truly seem to have emerged straight from the 1950s, are a fun option if you want to travel overnight to Moscow, Warsaw,

Prague, St. Petersburg, or Kiev. Compartments have two or four beds. For complete privacy, take one of these and pay for the spare bed or beds. Alternatively, join a four-berth and try chatting with your companions. Compartments for "women only" are offered on a few Minsk–Moscow trains. For those on a tight budget, normal seating is available, although hardly conducive to sleep. Buy tickets directly from the main train station or book through any Minsk travel agent.

WHERE TO STAY

The capital has few luxury hotels at present, although several more are currently being planned. The centrally located four-star Minsk Hotel is modern and pleasant, with doubles for around US $200 a night. The four-star Victoria Hotel charges a little less but is a half-hour walk from the center. The far less glamorous Hotel Belarus, near the picturesque old town, offers an alternative for around half the price. The five-star Europe Hotel, near October Square, is the most deluxe option, with prices to match (www.hoteleurope.by). Its Toni&Guy salon is a safe option for ladies' hairdressing. The five-star Crowne Plaza Hotel is also central, near Dynamo football stadium (around US $350). Keep expectations low for accommodation outside Minsk. Most hotels are shabby relics of Soviet times. The easiest way to book rooms is through a travel agent.

CURRENCY

There are plenty of state-regulated currency exchange booths, often found in underpasses or tucked inside the smarter shops. They also appear as little "vans" on 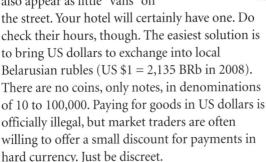 the street. Your hotel will certainly have one. Do check their hours, though. The easiest solution is to bring US dollars to exchange into local Belarusian rubles (US $1 = 2,135 BRb in 2008). There are no coins, only notes, in denominations of 10 to 100,000. Paying for goods in US dollars is officially illegal, but market traders are often willing to offer a small discount for payments in hard currency. Just be discreet.

ATMs, Credit Cards, and Traveler's Checks

There are a growing number of ATMs in the capital. Centrally, you'll find one inside GUM department store on Nezavisimosti and one in the Hotel Minsk. Credit cards are not yet widely accepted in shops and restaurants. Even where they are, it may be prudent not to hand them over because of the risk of fraud. Check with your hotel in advance that they are willing to accept a credit card payment (and be prepared to pay in dollars or rubles if they change their mind). Traveler's checks are not generally recognized but can be exchanged in larger banks, for a charge.

HEALTH

From October to April you'll need really warm clothes to go out in. Temperatures are often below 14°F (-10°C), and can even drop to -22°F (-30°C); without adequate protection this is extremely uncomfortable. Anyone walking on the street without a proper coat, hat, scarf, and gloves in winter will be chided by old ladies as foolhardy. The weather at other times is temperamental. Bring a light raincoat for summer (May to September), as it can be quite wet.

Belarusians are very careful with their health, to the point of hypochondria. They dislike drafts, as you will find out if you try to open a window for some fresh air! They are also suspicious of air-conditioning. At the merest hint of a cold, they dose themselves with various concoctions and, often, take the day off work. According to official statements, 80 percent of the population have health problems, ranging from vitamin deficiencies due to poor diet (too much starch and not enough protein) to thyroid cancer. Alcoholism is a major issue, and is being tackled by government health campaigns. Additionally, many Belarusians are still avid smokers.

Health Ministry reports show that Belarusians consult doctors 12.4 times a year on average, as against five to seven times for EU residents. Similarly, the hospital admission rate is 26.4 per 100 residents annually—two or three times higher than the rate in well-developed countries.

Few vaccinations are vital for your stay. If you are coming in summer, and may venture into the countryside, tick-borne encephalitis is a risk from small ticks that attach themselves to your legs in long grass. You can be immunized against this. It does no harm to be vaccinated against rabies, hepatitis A and B, tetanus, and typhoid.

When eating out, check that pork and chicken are properly cooked through, as undercooked meat is the commonest cause of stomach upsets. Pharmacies are stocked with soothing remedies.

Medical Facilities

The Belarusians enjoy free health care, with clinics in every suburb and town. Doctors tend to be well trained (albeit with some rather old-fashioned ideas) and the patient-to-doctor ratio is among the best in Europe. However, hospitals often lack modern equipment. As a foreigner, you are obliged to purchase health insurance on entry (unless you

are a resident diplomat) but this entitles you only
to basic care. Any problems that can wait until
your return are best endured. Be careful in winter,
when icy pavements make slipping a daily hazard;
it's easy to break a bone. You may prefer to seek
care in Vilnius, two and a half hours' drive from
Minsk. If you do wish to see a Belarusian doctor,
pay for private treatment. English is not widely
spoken, so take an interpreter with you.

Radioactivity
Since Chernobyl, visitors to Belarus are likely to be
concerned about radioactivity. During summer,
forest fires burn contaminated forests, throwing
radioactive material into the atmosphere. If you are
spending a short time in the country, the consensus
seems to be that you are unlikely to suffer lasting
damage. Opinion on longer-term residency is
divided. To play safe, avoid mushrooms, berries,
dairy products, and river fish, since these are
thought to absorb radioactivity most easily.
Although food originating in affected areas is not
supposed to be sold, it can be difficult to determine
where produce has been grown, especially in the
markets. Additionally, although food is supposed to
be randomly checked for radioactivity, and is
usually judged to be "satisfactory," you must decide
whether you are happy to eat it.

HIV
Very few Belarusians are officially registered as
being infected with HIV (just 10.1 per 100,000 in

2005). Men account for 68.1 percent of such cases and 69 percent of infections are thought to result from sharing needles when injecting drugs. Most of the affected are in their twenties.

SAFETY

Always carry your passport on you (the police may ask to see your documents), but keep a photocopy back at the hotel.

The crime rate is phenomenally low in Belarus. You are unlikely to feel threatened in any way, even alone late at night. However, it's sensible to take the usual precautions. After midnight, jump in a taxi if one is available and don't flash your cash unnecessarily. Pickpockets have been known to operate on the Metro, but they tend to go for easy targets such as an open bag or purse.

Men, beware of girls asking you back to their apartments. You don't know who might be waiting for you there. There are tales of foreign men arriving at the airport hoping to meet their Internet girlfriend, only to be met by her "brother." The unsuspecting Casanova finds himself dumped in a remote spot minus passport, money, and luggage.

DESTINATIONS

Belarus's monotonously flat marshland, studded with forest, may be unremarkable compared with the mountainous glory of Switzerland, Austria, Romania, or Bulgaria, and its lakes in no way compare with those of Italy, but Belarus has its own pristine charm. Its countryside and provincial areas are still largely unvisited by foreigners so, if you don't mind roughing it a little, you can reap the rewards of taking the path less traveled—a rare find in modern-day Europe. The Belarusian government is eager to attract tourists, so facilities countrywide are gradually improving.

The Brest Region
Belarus's main attraction is the Belovezhskaya Pushcha, Europe's last old-growth forest. This UNESCO-listed biosphere reserve is rich in wildlife and is home to three hundred bison (*zubr*). Polish Kings and Russian Tsars hunted there for centuries; in later years high-ranking

Soviet leaders, including Brezhnev, followed suit. It's a good spot for bird-watching. The other well-known Pushcha resident is Ded Moroz (Grandfather Frost). His charming "village" is open to tourists all year-round.

Just down the road from Hotel Visculi is the state residence where, in 1991, the leaders of Russia, Belarus, and Ukraine signed their agreement to dissolve the Soviet Union, creating the Commonwealth of Independent States (CIS).

In the town of Kamanets is the thirteenth-century White Tower, which you can climb to take in the wonderful view from the roof. Brest was the first Soviet town to confront the German army, in June 1941. The soldiers in the fortress endured a monthlong siege; many were shot while trying to drink from the river just a few yards away. The monument to the thirsty soldier and an immense stone soldier's head, entitled "Valor," are striking. Bullet holes remain in the red walls of the fortress.

The Gomel Region

The southeastern part of Belarus is very picturesque, with numerous lakes fed by the Dnieper, Sozh, Berezina, and Pripyat Rivers, and a third of its land covered by forest. It is also the most widely affected by radiation (more than 60 percent of its territory). The city of Gomel is second only to Minsk (population 500,000).

The Grodno Region

The attractive city of Grodno boasts old and new castles, and Pokrovsky and Farny Cathedrals on Sovietskaya Square. Having survived the war largely unscathed, it retains many more of its original beautiful old buildings.

The Minsk Region

For a taste of Belarus's historical heritage, drive a couple of hours out of Minsk to the ancient castles of Mir and Nesvizh. Mir is a sixteenth-century stone and red brick fortress with five formidable towers enclosing a spacious courtyard. Knights' tournaments are held in summer.

Nesvizh is a thirteenth-century castle built on an island. See the stunning baroque frescoes in nearby Corpus Christi Church, and venture into the dusty crypt. Lake Naroch and the Blue Lakes are pleasant places to relax; the local spa offers massages and a variety of therapies.

The Mogilev Region

President Lukashenko was born in the village of Shklov. The city of Mogilev dates back to the twelfth century, but little remains. There are the ruins of its sixteenth-century castle; worth a visit are St. Nicholas's monastery, the Cathedral of the Three Sanctifiers, and St. Stanislav's Cathedral. Mogilev hosts two annual music festivals: one in November and the other in July / August.

Black Barbara—A Belarusian Ghost Story

In 1547, the Grand Duke of Lithuania and heir to the throne of Poland, Sigismund Augustus, was secretly married to Barbara Radziwill, a beautiful Lithuanian Calvinist. In 1551, five months after her coronation, she suddenly died; it was widely believed that she had been poisoned by her mother-in-law, Bona Sforza. In desperation, Sigismund invited the sorcerer Pan Twardowski to conjure up the spirit of his dead wife. The sorcerer warned Sigismund not to touch or speak to the ghost, but, on seeing his beloved wife's apparition, he was overcome with emotion and ran toward her, calling her name. Since then, Barbara's ghost, dressed all in black, has walked the grounds of Nesvizh Castle at dusk. She is said to appear to young couples and those without children to wish them well and bring them strength.

The Vitebsk Region

Marc Chagall was born in Vitebsk in 1887, and called it his "second Paris." Despite being full of reproductions, the Marc Chagall Museum is very popular. In late July/early August, the town hosts an international song festival, the Slavonic Bazaar. Thousands of visitors flock to attend its open-air concerts, and rooms and tickets need to be booked several months in advance. Polotsk, Belarus's oldest town (first mentioned in 862), is blessed with St. Efrasinnia's Monastery, founded in 1125, and the eleventh-century Sofia Cathedral.

chapter eight

BUSINESS BRIEFING

THE BUSINESS ENVIRONMENT

Belarus was a major industrial center within the USSR. Following independence, the market for its goods disappeared, and it has had an uphill climb to reestablish itself. In 2006, it ranked second among the ten former Soviet states in the Commonwealth of Independent States for industrial output growth (11.3 percent), according to the CIS Statistics Committee.

However, Belarus has been receiving heavily discounted oil and natural gas from Russia. This

effectively subsidized the economy, and much of its growth can be attributed to the reexport of Russian oil at market prices. This growth is now threatened since Russia has raised energy prices for Belarus, bringing them more in line with the global market. Belarusian manufacturers are going to find it harder than ever to produce their goods at competitive prices.

The early years of independence were marked by soaring inflation; this has now been reduced to 10 percent, via tight administrative controls over prices and currency exchange rates. State-controlled salaries have been steadily raised at a rate exceeding that of GDP growth.

GDP has risen steadily since 1996. According to IMF figures, it stood at almost US $37 billion in 2006, compared to around US $341 billion in Poland and US $106 billion in Ukraine. Eighty percent of enterprises remain under state ownership, as does much property, giving the state great influence over production and employment. Unemployment was an amazingly low 1.3 percent in 2006, largely due to mass employment by the state; however, many are inefficiently "underemployed" at work.

In early 2007, Belarus's major trading partner was Russia, accounting for 48.1 percent of exports and imports. Together, the Netherlands, Germany, Ukraine, Poland, Latvia, Italy, and the UK accounted for 29.9 percent. China accounted for just 2.4 percent of trade and the USA for 2.3 percent. In 2007, 17.5 percent of firms were in the red, and companies are now being encouraged to adopt modern management and marketing techniques to achieve competitiveness. In the first quarter of 2008, the foreign trade balance was positive, totalling $33.4m —a great improvement on the deficit of US $1.07 billion in mid-2007.

FOREIGN INVESTMENT

In the mid 1990s, when the President launched "market socialism," there had been little industrial modernization. Efforts are now being made to redress this, since Belarusian manufactures were becoming less and less competitive. In 2008, Prime Minister Sergey Sidorsky announced a drive for efficiency, innovation, and the creation of new

enterprises. Foreign investment will play a vital role in this process, and the authorities are eager to encourage joint ventures. The state has wide-ranging powers to intervene in the management of all enterprises, however, so it is important for firms to read the small print of their contracts carefully.

Belarus ranked fiftieth for its potential for attracting direct foreign investment in the UN's 2006 World Investment Report. In 2006, Foreign Direct Investment stood at US $14.1 million, compared to US $452.28 million in Lithuania, US $1.91 billion in Ukraine, and US $6.77 billion in Poland.

In order to encourage foreign investment, Free Economic Zones have been set up in Brest, Gomel, Minsk, Mogilev, and Vitbesk, offering preferential taxation rates for high-tech industries. Materials can be brought in without paying customs duties. However, most manufactures must be exported rather than sold domestically. Companies in the zone are exempt from nationalization or requisition.

THE LEGAL SYSTEM

Legislation governing business can still be ambiguous and inconsistent. Businesses face the inconvenience of frequently changing regulations, a complex system of permits, and rigorous inspections. International Finance Corporation (IFC) reports show that large numbers of businesses have had to resort to "persuasive payments" in order to function. Accordingly, Belarus has had trouble attracting foreign investment, which remains low. Foreign (and local) entrepreneurs are obliged to spend large amounts of money on consultants, lawyers, and accountants, endeavoring to navigate the system. The IFC has had some success in convincing the authorities to simplify the bureaucracy involved in setting up and operating small and medium-sized businesses; but there is still a great way to go.

FUTURE PROSPECTS

Belarus has long relied on Russia as its main trading partner. However, the relationship seems to be growing more strained, with Putin indicating that, in future, Russia will not be willing to prop up the Belarusian economy with subsidized gas and oil sales. Negotiations are continuing. Trade with EU partners has been growing steadily, with Germany and the Netherlands taking the lead.

Most enterprises remain state-owned, with restrictions placed on foreign ownership of property and land. Budget funding is being set aside to modernize industrial plants.

Some efforts have been made to reform the complexity of the tax, permit, and inspection systems, but they remain a minefield.

Young people are generally well educated but are often frustrated by the lack of opportunities at home. Working abroad remains an attractive prospect to many.

BUSINESS CULTURE
Soviet Legacy and Aspirations

The Soviet legacy shows itself in a general reluctance to take responsibility for decisions. Long-term centralist planning remains, with traditional "Soviet" five-year plans. State-run enterprises remain slow to respond to market needs, although the government is making efforts to encourage innovation. Membership in the Belarusian Republican Youth Union (the new Komsomol) does no harm to one's career, while those who become involved in opposition party activities may find that this adversely affects their career prospects. Nepotism is widespread.

The system encourages "over-employment;" as a consequence, many people don't have enough to do and lack ambition. Many offices and factories are rather run-down, with peeling paint, rotten windows, and unpleasant restrooms, and foster apathy. Work is generally seen as a means to an end rather than a pleasure in itself.

Factories and farms sometimes employ a reward system to encourage productivity. As in Soviet times, the "best" workers may have their photos displayed each month and be awarded a cash bonus. At harvest time, those who have collected the most crops even appear on prime-time TV to collect congratulatory prizes. This system is some way from other countries' notions of performance-related pay, however.

Micro-Management

A foreign delegation came to visit the president. Halfway through their talk they were interrupted by an urgent call for the premier. They could hear him saying, "Yes, Yes, No—not that one, Yes, Yes—that's fine, No—that one's no good." When the call ended they asked what he'd been advising on. "Oh," he replied in exasperation, "It was one of my farm managers. He wanted me to approve the potato crop!"

The Importance of Personal Relationships

These cannot be stressed too highly. Your Belarusian contacts won't be interested in pursuing business with you unless they feel they can get along with you. Trust is earned through traditional bonding via the *banya* and a spot of vodka. Belarusians can detect insincerity a mile off, so remain genuine and don't make promises you can't keep.

MEETINGS

Making Contact

Belarusian companies attend several international trade fairs to promote their goods. You can find a schedule on the Chamber of Commerce Web site (www.cci.by/en/PageE1.html). This organization is an excellent source of information, and will help introduce you to appropriate companies with which to liaise.

Etiquette

Punctuality isn't a Belarusian forte, and meetings may be cancelled at the last minute. You can only be patient and allow yourself plenty of flexibility. Take these frustrations with good grace.

Older Belarusians may introduce themselves by their first name and patronymic (see Chapter 4, Making Friends: Names and Introductions). Use both until they tell you to do otherwise—it's a sign of respect. Since you don't have a patronymic, they'll call you by your first name. Younger people will only expect you to use their first names. After some time, they may show familiarity by asking you to use their diminutive name, for example, Alexander might ask you to call him Sasha.

Shake hands with everyone, including late arrivals, and offer your business card to every person present (English on one side and Russian on the other is usual). A good job title is necessary; your partners will want to be assured they are dealing with someone of importance.

Your experience will differ greatly depending on whether you are liaising with private businessmen or with officials running a state-owned company. If you are meeting the former, you'll probably be liaising directly with the top managers or even the owners themselves. It's unlikely they'll arrange a morning meeting. An appointment over lunch (around 2:00 p.m.) or dinner (around 7:00 p.m.) is likely, although you might be invited to their office for refreshments instead. Your first meeting will be a "getting to know you" occasion: you'll be asked about your journey, your family, your home city, and what you think of Belarus. Be open, sincere, and honest, but avoid making any negative remarks about your host country—it won't be appreciated. Your hosts will want to decide whether they like and trust you, and if they can foresee working with you. Exaggerated smiling or effusiveness will seem false.

Follow the usual rules of polite society: accept any food or drink offered to you, and pretend to like it even if you don't. A bottle of vodka may be produced, and it's traditional that it is drunk neat and to the last drop; just make sure you also take the water and finger food provided and you should come away unscathed. In some cases, this initial stage may include a trip to a *banya*, a traditional meeting place for businessmen (see Chapter 6, Time Out: The *Banya*). Additionally, you'll be given a tour, for example of the factory premises.

If you will be dealing with state officials, you can expect the meetings to be a great deal more formal. They'll open your first meeting with the usual pleasantries, but will soon get down to business. The level of manager sent to meet you will depend on the size of your own company and the scope of the deal you are proposing. If all goes well, higher managers will be brought in later on.

From the outset, employ a good local interpreter. Not only will they navigate the language for you, they'll know the format of the proceedings and can tell you what to expect. Once negotiations begin in earnest, ask them to take notes for you as your record of what's been agreed.

Presentations

Belarus is now starting to move with the times, so be prepared to bring a laptop with you, such as for a Microsoft PowerPoint presentation. Naturally, sales and growth figures are essential. Keep your pitch straightforward; the simpler your rhetoric, the more sincere you will appear. Color brochures and samples of your company's products are invaluable.

Your audience will listen politely, but be ready for acute questions when you open the floor. The Belarusians will be shrewd and to the point, and will expect you to have answers.

Your new partners will want to take away all the materials you have offered for careful private study and discussion. They'll then contact you for further meetings if they are interested.

NEGOTIATION

Belarusians are reasonable and pragmatic. During the negotiation stage, your partners will state their requirements succinctly and will expect you to do the same. You don't need to play games or employ psychological tactics, but do expect tough negotiation and compromise. In the early stages, the signing of a "Protocol of Intent" is usual: this is a memorandum laying down guidelines for your future contract. It's not legally binding, so details can still be changed.

The next stage is to draw up a draft agreement stating the terms and conditions you propose. They'll do the same, and these can be exchanged for private discussion. A further meeting can then be used to thrash out the finer points. Make sure you have a legal representative to look over everything.

CONTRACTS AND FULFILLMENT

Once the final contract has been agreed (usually including a penalty clause for late delivery) you'll meet to sign it and celebrate your new relationship, though sometimes the celebration will be postponed until your first payment or delivery arrives. Such celebrations are an essential part of your relationship. Remember, signing a contract is only the start.

The implementation phase is likely to be complicated by customs problems, the need for state approvals and various other legislative obstacles. Patience and persistence are required on both sides. Your personal relationship will again be tested. Even though your contract may stipulate specific details, e.g. fixed prices for fixed amounts of goods or services, be ready for flexibility. Your local liaison may need additional payments from you to help them navigate their way through Belarusian bureaucracy.

RENTING BUSINESS SPACE

Business rentals are escalating in price (up by 16 percent in 2007), due to a shortage of desirable properties and rising costs for new building construction. Office rents in Minsk far exceed those found in neighboring capitals, while standards leave something to be desired. Monthly rents of 35 to 40 euros per square meter are common, while similar properties in Warsaw might cost 10 euros. The best offices are in centrally located new or refurbished buildings and include car parking, Internet connections, restrooms, and some kitchen facilities.

Warehouses and manufacturing premises are also in short supply and cost around 10 euros per square meter (excluding utilities)—double the price of those in Riga and Warsaw. If using a property agency, pay commission only when a suitable building has been signed over to you.

WOMEN IN BUSINESS

During Soviet times, women were expected to run the household, bring up children, and have jobs. They often relied on their own mothers to help out. Little has changed in modern Belarus. The aftermath of the Second World War upset the male:female ratio of the population, and women were called on to help restore the economy. Having a career has become the norm, but motherhood, as we have seen, is still a "sacred duty." Women are paid around 20 percent less than men with the same or better qualifications. They comprise 67 percent of white-collar workers and dominate the teaching and medical professions. However, they are underrepresented in senior business roles and in parliament. In a bid to encourage childbearing to counteract the declining population, the state grants 126 days of maternity leave (140 days in cases of medical complications). Additionally, women's jobs must be held open (unpaid) for their return for up to three years. If another child is born in this time, the three-year allowance begins anew. It is perhaps not surprising that many employers are wary of taking on young women in key positions.

chapter nine

COMMUNICATING

Limerick
County Library

RUSSIAN VERSUS BELARUSIAN

Belarusian is an East Slavic language, closely

related to Russian and Ukrainian, but with many similarities to Polish. About 7.5 million people in Belarus speak it, most of whom are bilingual in Belarusian and Russian. "Old Belarusian" was the official language of the Grand Duchy of Lithuania from the thirteenth century until 1696. It was initially written in Cyrillic script and was heavily influenced by Church Slavonic, the liturgical language of the Orthodox Church.

The first book to be printed in an East Slavic language was a Belarusian translation of the Psalter, printed in Prague in 1517 by the Renaissance scholar Francisk Skoryna (born in Polotsk c. 1490). An alumnus of Krakow and Padua universities, Skoryna translated the Bible into vernacular Old Belarusian, thus laying the foundations of literary Belarusian. Between 1517 and 1519 he printed twenty-three books of the

Bible with his own commentaries and prefaces. Although he was probably Roman Catholic, this Bible came to be used by Belarusian Orthodox believers. In 1520 he founded a printing press in Vilnius, where he continued his work.

During the sixteenth century, handwritten Belarusian texts started to appear in the Latin alphabet, although by 1710 Old Belarusian had been replaced by Polish as the official language of the state. During the late nineteenth century, Belarusian, written in the Latin alphabet, started to emerge as a literary language closer to its modern form, despite Tsarist measures to instill the use of Cyrillic only. In the early twentieth century both alphabets were used. Between the wars, Cyrillic became the official alphabet of the Soviet Socialist Republic of Byelorussia, while in Polish western Belarus both alphabets continued to coexist. The Soviet Union's Russification policy in the 1960s made Russian the standard language of education, government, and business.

When Belarus declared independence in August 1991, it reinstated Belarusian as the sole official language. However, in 1995, a cooperative pact was signed with Russia officially giving the two languages equal status.

In fact, Russian is far more widely spoken and printed in Belarus, and is the main language of education. In 2006, only 18.6 percent of first-year schoolchildren were being taught through the medium of Belarusian. In most schools, Belarusian is relegated to a few hours of lessons a week. The Belarusian Language Society continues to petition for its greater recognition. In fact, support for reinstating Belarusian as the national language is closely associated with support for the opposition—which is against the formation of the Union State with Russia.

Unlike Russian, the Belarusian language version of the Cyrillic alphabet does not use the letter "Ë" (but "¥") and does not use the diacritic mark "˜" at all; additionally, it uses "Ÿ" for our "w" sound (absent in Russian).

Some Belarusian words do use the same stem as their Russian counterparts, so if you know Russian you can take a stab at a translation. Some words are quite different.

SOME USEFUL PHRASES		
	Russian	**Belarusian**
Hello	*Privyet*	*Vitayu*
Pleased to meet you	*Ochin priatna*	*Pryiemna paznajomicca*
Thank you	*Spasiba*	*Dziakuy*
Please	*Pajalasta*	*Kali laska*
I don't understand	*Ni panimayu*	*Ne razumeyu*

FORMAL AND INFORMAL ADDRESS

Russian uses two forms of address: the familiar second person (*ty*) for addressing children and close friends, and the polite second person (*vy*).

Always use the latter when meeting new people (unless they are very young) and continue using it until invited to use the familiar—a sign that your relationship is growing warmer.

If you need to call over a waitress, you can address her as *Dyevushka* (young lady). More than likely she'll ignore you, but it's worth a go. A waiter can be addressed as *Malodoi chyelovyek* (young man). You can use these words to address young adults you don't know, for example when asking directions. There is no such suitable form of address for older adults—just ask with a smile, a please, and a thank you.

HUMOR

Belarusians love to tease each other. The more acute the teasing, the stronger the friendship. They also enjoy laughing at themselves. Their sense of humor ranges from the dark and intellectual to slapstick (the predominant feature of TV entertainment). Jokes relating to the political situation abound, but are shared only behind closed doors in trusted company.

As in Soviet times, people are still aware that openly telling a political joke could land them in trouble. Don't be tempted to tell such jokes yourself, as it will be construed as inappropriate or even rude. Foreigners aren't expected to be conversant with the complexities of the local situation. To offer an opinion is ignorant at best, arrogant at worst.

Laughing at Themselves

Belarusians can laugh at their own traditional passivity. They have a history of putting up with unpleasantness, believing that trials are sent to be endured rather than fought against.

An American, a Russian, and a Belarusian are asked in turn to sit on a chair that has a thumbtack on it. The American sits down first and, on feeling the thumbtack, springs up again, with a "Damn it!" The Russian also quickly jumps up, uttering a four-letter word. The Belarusian then sits down and feels the thumbtack pierce his flesh. His first inclination is to move, but he just settles down, and says, "Perhaps it should be so."

. . . and at Life Under the KGB

Two Belarusian KGB officers are traveling on a train, telling each other political jokes. "Hold on a second, I need to change my tape," says one. "Don't bother, you can copy mine later," says the other.

SWEARING

Russian is said to have more swearwords than any other language in the world. However, Belarusians tend not to use strong curses in polite company; it would be thought uncouth. One of the mildest local expletives is *chort*, which literally means "devil," but is used as the equivalent of "damn." Amusingly, it's nearly always used in the Russian subtitling of movies, regardless of the strength of the English curse uttered on screen. You may also hear the occasional stronger English swearword uttered within a torrent of Russian. Although this may shock, Belarusians don't have a feeling for the strength of English swearwords.

BODY LANGUAGE AND PERSONAL SPACE

Personal space here is much smaller than you may be comfortable with. On the metro, in shops, and even on the street people will rub shoulders with you, jostling or bumping you as they pass. This is part of the Soviet legacy, when pushing forward was the best way to get what you needed. It may alarm you at first, but you will soon get used to it and find yourself doing the same!

Sympathetic Magic

Once, telling a story, I drew my finger across my neck to indicate death. My Belarusian companion was horrified. Using a hand gesture in this way is thought to encourage evil spirits to make the action real—so I was wishing decapitation on myself. To remedy my action, my friend "grabbed" the bad energy from around my neck and "threw it away."

Keep your hands out of your pockets when speaking to people, and be ready to shake hands with everyone. It is impolite to point with your finger—use your whole hand instead. Flicking your neck with your fingers suggests either "Let's get drunk" or, when indicating others, that they are already tipsy. Twisting your finger at your temple while inclining your head toward others indicates that you think them crazy.

SERVICES
Telephone and Fax

Neither cell phone nor fixed line coverage is yet universal: some rural areas are still waiting for such services to reach them. The state-owned Beltelcom is currently modernizing its landline network, and gradually switching to digital.

Payphones are easy to find in major cities but most can't be used for international calls; you'll need to go to a large post office. These only accept special phone cards (not cash or credit or debit cards), which are sold at post offices and newspaper kiosks.

Expect half of the calls you receive to be wrong numbers. Moreover, your own mystery callers won't identify themselves. They'll either hang up without a word once you speak or will persist in asking for Irina, Tanya, or Oleg, regardless of your protestations.

There has been a cell phone explosion in Belarus. Certainly, those who can afford to do so like to update their cell phone handset regularly, treating it as a fashion accessory and status symbol.

The market is thought to be almost saturated already, and providers are now concentrating on persuading users to upgrade to more sophisticated models and more comprehensive packages. Phone charges are comparatively low: around US $0.10 to 20 per minute for a local call from a cell phone, and less on a landline. Making international calls from your Belarusian cell phone costs around US $0.70 per minute, compared to US $0.50 on a fixed line. Of course, hotels charge far more if you phone from your room. You may be able to use your existing GSM phone within Belarus if you have a roaming option, but check beforehand what charges may apply, or you could have an unpleasant shock. It is possible to rent a cell phone: see www.velcom.by, www.belcel.by or www.mts.by.

Large post offices and hotels have fax services.

DIALING CODES

The international code for Belarus is 375.

The code for Minsk is 17.

To phone between cities in Belarus (or within CIS), press 8, then the city code, then the individual number.

To call abroad from Belarus (outside CIS), press 8, then 10, then the country code, the city code, and the number.

Internet and E-mail

Many people still don't have Internet access from home (or a computer, for that matter) and, as yet, Internet cafés are few and far between, even in

Minsk. Much progress has been made, though. According to a UNO report, in early 2006, a third of the population was regularly using the Net. International Telecommunication Union figures for 2007 placed the figure at 56.6 percent—a huge leap from 14.3 percent in 2003. Internet cafés can be found centrally at 8 Nemiga Street (Nemiga metro), at 58 Nezavisimosti (Y. Kolas metro), and at 3 Krasnoarmeiskaya Street (October Square metro). Don't be surprised if you are asked to register before using the terminals. The government is keen to keep a log of who has been accessing what sites. When you do get online, you'll find that connections are often slow, so surfing the Web can be frustrating; you may also find some "controversial" sites (such as the unofficial opposition site Charter 97) are blocked. Minsk's newest hotels are being fitted with business centers, so guests will be able to dial up from them, and some public areas, such as Minsk's train station, are being fitted for wireless connection.

Mail
Belpochta (www.belpost.by/default2.htmis) is the state-run mail service, with branches in every suburb and small town. Here, you can pay your utility bills, send money orders, access the Internet, make international phone calls, collect benefits and pensions, and access savings accounts, as well as buying stationery and mailing letters. The state mail service is

reasonably reliable but slow. Courier services are a much better bet. You can DHL into and out of Minsk.

THE MEDIA
Radio and TV

Local TV channels and radio stations are state controlled. If you are staying in one of the more modern hotels, you may have satellite TV channels. For some years, there has been legislation requiring radio services to broadcast 85 percent Belarusian music. Needless to say, this has been a challenge; quotas are usually achieved by playing the same tracks through the night. You'll also hear a mixture of Russian pop and American and European hits on most stations. Some radio stations over the border broadcast into Belarus, offering alternatives.

Newspapers and Magazines

Many state-run Russian-language papers are in circulation. *Belarus Segodnya* tops sales, largely due to mandatory subscription by all state-run workplaces. This sociopolitical daily runs stories on sporting, cultural, academic, and economic achievements to promote a positive image of Belarus. The second-most popular paper is *Komsomolskaya Pravda v Belarusi*, a regional edition of the Moscow-based *Komsomolskaya Pravda*.

In theory, independent printed media are available. Sadly, the independent press has been forced into closure on receiving huge state fines for various violations. In October 2005, the state-owned monopoly printers and distributors terminated the contract of the last remaining independent daily newspaper, *Narodnaya Volya*. At the start of 2006, the state-owned postal service refused to distribute several remaining small independent editions; some have now set up just over the border, but cars are regularly searched as they cross checkpoints and such editions are confiscated, with drivers receiving significant fines. Imported Western newspapers are not available, so the Internet offers the most comprehensive coverage of international news.

The two state-run weekly English-language newspapers—*Belarus Today* and the *Minsk Times*—are available from Belarusian embassies worldwide and on Belavia airline flights. You can pick up *Where Minsk* (Russian and English text) at most of the smarter restaurants. This covers cultural events, has a large business address guide at the back, and prints some interesting articles on local trends. *Minsk In Your Pocket*, a lighthearted guide, is also available in print and online.

CONCLUSION

Belarus is heading for a key moment in its history. Will it relegate its Soviet past to the bonfire and turn westward toward the EU, or will it continue to nestle under the wing of Russia? The Belarusian and Russian leadership continues to pay little more than lip service to the concept of a Union State, neither being willing to compromise. The question remains, however, whether Belarus will be subsumed economically into its "older brother." The current leadership looks confident of staying in power for years. Indeed, many would say that the opposition needs to show itself to be a great deal more assertive and organized before it can be seen as a viable alternative.

Belarus's future remains in the balance. Lukashenko sees China, Cuba, Iran, North Korea, Sudan, Syria, and Venezuela as his strong supporters against outside influences. The EU is keen to see the development of a modern, democratic, and free Belarus on its border. It also wants to ensure security for gas and oil supplies, which transit the country. However, it believes Belarus's approach to human rights, democracy, good governance, the independent media, and civil society is in sore need of reform: this is a country where defaming the president or members of his government (or indeed committing an action deemed "oppositionist") is an offense punishable by imprisonment.

The majority of Belarusians have limited opportunities for travel, so their vision of the world is gleaned mainly from state media. As a result, most remain blissfully ignorant of alternatives to the life they currently lead. Their most common comparison is between Minsk and

Moscow. They perceive the latter as noisy, expensive, dirty, and dangerous, and ravaged by the worst excesses of capitalism, albeit with a better selection of shops and cafés. Meanwhile, their beloved Minsk is familiar, friendly, clean, quiet, and safe. At times, you might even feel inclined to agree with them.

Visitors to Belarus will find much that is strange and frustrating. Life for most Belarusians is harder than it is elsewhere. However, they make the best of their circumstances, and take true joy in their friends and family. The Belarusians are remarkable for their kindness, warmth, friendliness, and sincerity. Few who travel to Belarus fail to return time and time again.

Further Reading

Chagall, Marc. *My Life*. New York: 1st Da Capo Press, 1960.

Duffy, Peter. *Bielski Brothers*. New York: Harper Perennial, 2004.

Feeley, F.M. *And the Wisdom to Know the Difference, Conversations with Residents of San Francisco, Paris and Minsk*. Quebec: World Heritage Press, 1998.

Ioffe, Grigory. *Understanding Belarus and How Western Foreign Policy Misses the Mark*. Lanham, Maryland: Rowman & Littlefield, 2008.

Jackson, Jackson. *Joseph Gavi: Young Hero of the Minsk Ghetto*. Paducah, Kentucky: Turner Publishing Company, 2000.

Marples, David. *Belarus: From Soviet Rule to Nuclear Catastrophe*. New York: St. Martin's Press, 1996.

Parker, Stewart. *The Last Soviet Republic: Alexander Lukashenko's Belarus*. Victoria, British Columbia, Canada: Trafford Publishing, 2007.

Roberts, Nigel. *Belarus*. Chalfont St. Peter, Buckinghamshire, UK: Bradt Travel Guides, 2008.

Alexievich, Svetlana (trans. Keith Gessen). *Voices from Chernobyl: The Oral History of a Nuclear Disaster*. New York: St. Martin's Press, 2006.

For a lighthearted view, see the "In Your Pocket Guide to Minsk," available for download free of charge at www.inyourpocket.com/belarus/city/minsk

For a taste of state-run news, pick up a copy of the *Minsk Times*, a weekly edition available on Belavia airlines and at Belarusian Embassies worldwide.

To see what's on and where to go during your stay, read the *Where Minsk* city guide, a monthly edition widely available in the capital's hotels and restaurants.

Useful Web Sites

www.inyourpocket.com/country/belarus.html

General tourist information:
  www.belarustourism.by
  www.belarus.by
  www.belarusguide.com
  www.belarusembassy.org

Ministry of Foreign Affairs: www.mfa.gov.by/eng

Customs: www.customs.gov.by/en/

Chamber of Commerce: www.cci.by/en/PageE1.html

Political opposition : www.charter97.org/en/news/

Jewish cemeteries: www.jewishgen.org/cemetery/e-europe/belarus.html

culture smart! **belarus**

Index